FRUIT CHAN'S
Made in Hong Kong

Hong Kong University Press thanks Xu Bing for writing the Press's name in his Square Word Calligraphy for the covers of its books. For further information see p. iv.

THE NEW HONG KONG CINEMA SERIES

The New Hong Kong Cinema came into existence under very special circumstances, during a period of social and political crisis resulting in a change of cultural paradigms. Such critical moments have produced the cinematic achievements of the early Soviet cinema, neorealism, the *nouvelle vague*, and the German cinema of the 1970s and, we can now say, the New Hong Kong Cinema. If this cinema grew increasingly intriguing in the 1980s, after the announcement of Hong Kong's return to China, it is largely because it had to confront a new cultural and political space that was both complex and hard to define, where the problems of colonialism were uncannily overlaid with those of globalism. Such uncanniness could not be caught through straight documentary or conventional history writing: it was left to the cinema to define it.

Has the creative period of the New Hong Kong Cinema now come to an end? However we answer the question, there is a need to evaluate the achievements of Hong Kong cinema. This series distinguishes itself from the other books on the subject by focusing in-depth on individual Hong Kong films, which together make the New Hong Kong Cinema.

Series General Editors
Ackbar Abbas, Wimal Dissanayake, Mette Hjort, Gina Marchetti, Stephen Teo

Series Advisors
Chris Berry, Nick Browne, Ann Hui, Leo Lee, Li Cheuk-to, Patricia Mellencamp, Meaghan Morris, Paul Willemen, Peter Wollen, Wu Hung

Other titles in the series
Andrew Lau and Alan Mak's *Infernal Affairs – The Trilogy* by Gina Marchetti
Fruit Chan's *Durian Durian* by Wendy Gan
John Woo's *A Better Tomorrow* by Karen Fang
Jonn Woo's *Bullet in the Head* by Tony Williams
John Woo's *The Killer* by Kenneth E. Hall
Johnnie To Kei-fung's *PTU* by Michael Ingham
King Hu's *A Touch of Zen* by Stephen Teo
Mabel Cheung Yuen-ting's *An Autumn's Tale* by Stacilee Ford
Peter Ho-sun Chan's *He's a Woman, She's a Man* by Lisa Odham Stokes
Stanley Kwan's *Center Stage* by Mette Hjort
Tsui Hark's *Zu: Warriors From the Magic Mountain* by Andrew Schroeder
Wong Kar-wai's *Ashes of Time* by Wimal Dissanayake
Wong Kar-wai's *Happy Together* by Jeremy Tambling
Yuen Woo-ping's *Wing Chun* by Sasha Vojković

FRUIT CHAN'S
Made in Hong Kong

Esther M. K. Cheung

香港大學出版社
HONG KONG UNIVERSITY PRESS

Hong Kong University Press
14/F Hing Wai Centre
7 Tin Wan Praya Road
Aberdeen
Hong Kong

© Hong Kong University Press 2009

ISBN 978-962-209-977-7

British Library Cataloguing-in-Publication Data
A catalogue record for this book is available from the British Library.

Secure on-line Ordering
http://www.hkupress.org

Printed and bound by Pre-Press Ltd., Hong Kong, China

Hong Kong University Press is honoured that Xu Bing, whose art explores the complex themes of language across cultures, has written the Press's name in his Square Word Calligraphy. This signals our commitment to cross-cultural thinking and the distinctive nature of our English-language books published in China.

"At first glance, Square Word Calligraphy appears to be nothing more unusual than Chinese characters, but in fact it is a new way of rendering English words in the format of a square so they resemble Chinese characters. Chinese viewers expect to be able to read Square Word Calligraphy but cannot. Western viewers, however are surprised to find they can read it. Delight erupts when meaning is unexpectedly revealed."
— Britta Erickson, *The Art of Xu Bing*

To
Maria, Tom, and Sabrina

Table of Contents

Series Preface   ix

Acknowledgements   xiii

1   Introduction: History beyond the Death Trips   1

2   Authenticity and Independence: Fruit Chan and   21
      Independent Filmmaking

3   There Are Many Ways to Be Realistic   39

4   The Art of *Détournement*   53

5   In Search of the Ghostly in Context   79

6   In Search of the Ghostly in Urban Spaces   101

7   Epilogue: Grassrooting Cinematic Practices   125

Appendix 1: Interview with Fruit Chan   129

Appendix 2: Funding Sources and Awards   145

Notes   151

Credits   167

Bibliography   171

Series Preface

The New Hong Kong Cinema came into existence under very special circumstances, during a period of social and political crisis resulting in a change of cultural paradigms. Such critical moments have produced the cinematic achievements of the early Soviet cinema, neorealism, the *nouvelle vague*, the German cinema in the 1970s and, we can now say, the recent Hong Kong cinema. If this cinema grew increasingly intriguing in the 1980s, after the announcement of Hong Kong's return to China, it was largely because it had to confront a new cultural and political space that was both complex and hard to define, where the problems of colonialism were overlaid with those of globalism in an uncanny way. Such uncanniness could not be caught through straight documentary or conventional history writing; it was left to the cinema to define it.

It does so by presenting to us an urban space that slips away if we try to grasp it too directly, a space that cinema coaxes into existence by whatever means at its disposal. Thus it is by eschewing a narrow idea of relevance and pursuing disreputable genres like melodrama, kung fu and the fantastic that cinema brings into view something else about the city which could otherwise be missed. One classic example is Stanley Kwan's *Rouge*, which draws on the unrealistic form of the ghost story to evoke something of the uncanniness of Hong Kong's urban space. It takes a ghost to catch a ghost.

In the New Hong Kong Cinema, then, it is neither the subject matter nor a particular set of generic conventions that is paramount. In fact, many Hong Kong films begin by following generic conventions but proceed to transform them. Such transformation of genre is also the transformation of a sense of place where all the rules have quietly and deceptively changed. It is this shifting sense of place, often expressed negatively and indirectly — but in the best work always rendered precisely in (necessarily) innovative images — that is decisive for the New Hong Kong Cinema.

Has the creative period of the New Hong Kong Cinema come to an end? However we answer the question, there is a need now to evaluate the achievements of Hong Kong cinema. During the last few years, a number of full-length books have appeared, testifying to the topicality of the subject. These books survey the field with varying degrees of success, but there is yet an almost complete lack of authoritative texts focusing in depth on individual Hong Kong films. This book series on the New Hong Kong Cinema is designed to fill this lack. Each volume will be written by a scholar/ critic who will analyse each chosen film in detail and provide a critical apparatus for further discussion including filmography and bibliography.

Our objective is to produce a set of interactional and provocative readings that would make a self-aware intervention into modern Hong Kong culture. We advocate no one theoretical position; the authors will approach their chosen films from their own distinct points of vantage and interest. The aim of the series is to generate open-ended discussions of the selected films, employing diverse analytical strategies, in order to urge the readers towards self-reflective engagements with the films in particular and the Hong Kong cultural space in general. It is our hope that this series will contribute to the sharpening of Hong Kong culture's conceptions of itself.

In keeping with our conviction that film is not a self-enclosed signification system but an important cultural practice among similar others, we wish to explore how films both reflect and inflect culture. And it is useful to keep in mind that reflection of reality and reality of reflection are equally important in the understanding of cinema.

Ackbar Abbas
Wimal Dissanayake

Acknowledgements

The genesis of this book can be traced back to a moment of illumination. The familiar images of Hong Kong's public housing estates in Fruit Chan's *Made in Hong Kong* struck me as personal and spectral. They recalled childhood memories of residing in such grassroots locales. The moving resonances in these forgotten spaces metamorphosed for me over the years into a scholarly discourse on urban mutations and the condition of marginality.

During this process, the greatest enabler was Ackbar Abbas who not only inspired me intellectually but also introduced my work to Hong Kong University Press. His great insights on an earlier paper on the ghostly city helped me develop Chapters 5 and 6 in this book. Mette Hjort shared her views on different approaches to the study of emotion and globalization. Gina Marchetti's collegiality and encouragement have made the writing process an enjoyable and positive experience. Meaghan Morris and Stephen Chan supported me continuously and provided me with a chance to present parts of this research project at a Lingnan University conference. Markus Reisenleitner gave me valuable insights on architectural space and city culture. Susan Ingram's appreciation of my work and her invitation to the 2006 Congress of Canadian Comparative Literature Association (CCLA) Annual Meeting marked an important stage in the development of this project.

Colin Day and Michael Duckworth of Hong Kong University Press have supported this book with great patience and constant encouragement. I am thankful to Colin for providing speedy, professional help in the review process. Michael might not be aware of how much his appreciation has energized me. My heartfelt thanks go to his thoughtful and concrete suggestions for dealing with the revisions. I have benefited enormously from the anonymous reviewers who offered me precious advice through their meticulous and careful reading of the manuscript. My appreciation also goes to Dawn Lau for her meticulous proofreading of the manuscripts.

While this project has taken longer than expected, I have enjoyed working with my research assistants at various stages of the journey. Jamie Ku, Elaine Kwok, Cheng Kwok Hung, Nicole Hess, and Michelle Kwok contributed their precious time to support my endeavor. Michelle, in particular, has been a wonderful, endearing companion throughout the process. Her generosity, professional finesse, and whole-hearted dedication will always be remembered. My students, Jason Ho, Winnie Yee, Fiona Law, and Vicky Yau never refrained from cheering from the sidelines. Jason may not know how his faith in the project became such a sweet treat in bitter times.

Research for this book was completed with the generous support from two grants: "Seed Funding for Basic Research" of the University of Hong Kong and the "General Research Fund" of Research Grants Council of the Hong Kong Special Administrative Region, China (Project No. HKU 7416/05H). I also thank sincerely the Department of Comparative Literature at the University of Hong Kong for providing all the necessary institutional support.

Without Fruit Chan's generosity, this book would not have come into being. In the first instance, he shared in an interview his passionate pursuit of alternative practices at a *kairotic* time which became an indescribable motivating force for me to engage in cultural criticism as an afterlife for the film. He allowed use of the print and visual archive at Golden Network Asia, and generously granted permission to use Susan's ghostly rooftop image on the book cover. Lammy Li of Golden Network Asia has offered invaluable liaison help. I will never forget Shu Kei who provided me with the initial contact with Golden Network Asia and insights on the distribution of independent films in Hong Kong.

I dedicate this book to three beloved individuals in my life: my sister Maria, who shared with me her childhood in one of Hong Kong's vanished housing estates; Tom, who understands and appreciates so thoroughly my passions for this intellectual endeavor; and my little girl Sabrina, who was born the same year this remarkable film was made in Hong Kong.

Introduction:
History beyond the Death Trips

The imagination is always at the end of an era.

— Frank Kermode[1]

A typical story of disaffected youth and the morbid trips they take, *Made in Hong Kong* (1997) narrates the tale of four youngsters coming from the lower sector of Hong Kong society. Moon (Zhongqiu/Chung-chau), Ping (Ping/Ping), Sylvester (Long/Lung), and Susan (Shan/San) are all subject to the cruel realities of life in a big city.[2] Like many Hong Kong lower-class inhabitants, they reside in the public housing estates known for their dismal living conditions. Moon and Ping both grow up in families where irresponsible fathers have run away from home. Their mothers are neither courageous nor enduring. Sylvester, a mentally handicapped young man who is abandoned by his family and society, befriends Moon and Ping. The school girl Susan cannot bear the disillusionment which results from her failed romantic relationship with her teacher who shirks the responsibility of admitting their relationship, and commits suicide by jumping off the roof of a Hong Kong high-rise building. After Sylvester has picked up Susan's dead letters and has given them to Moon, the latter seems to be possessed and erotically aroused by Susan's ghost night after night. Ever since then, their deadly destinies are tied together. Sylvester ends up being killed by gangsters, Ping dies of an incurable kidney disease, and Moon commits suicide at the end of the film.

Now often hailed as a story about grassroots people by a "grassroots director," *Made in Hong Kong* excited both local viewers and international spectators as Fruit Chan's powerful independent debut in an eventful year.[3] In the history of world cinema, the disaffected youth is a well-recognized trope to refer to symptoms of the problems of contemporary cities. An effective figure in the tradition of social realism, this character suffers from urban alienation, economic inequality, the feeling of loss, and disorientation when one is coming of age as well as the predicament of being abandoned in the adult world. Like other films in this tradition, *Made in Hong Kong* is an indictment of a society where youth express their urban angst and disillusionment. While the "cruel tragedies of youth" are fundamental to any big city, they always embody local specificities.[4] The youngsters' death trips allegorize the concluding chapter of British colonial history in Hong Kong. Chan once said that their deaths signified the need to turn over a new leaf when Hong Kong re-entered China's political and cultural realities.[5] It is this allegorical reference to the 1997 handover that places the film in the category of "New Hong Kong Cinema."[6] The 1997 handover, as Walter Benjamin would have called it, is a "moment of danger" when filmic images "[flash] up at the instant when it can be recognized."[7] The trope of the disaffected youth merges the general condition of urban alienation with specific symptoms of a society at a historical moment of drastic transition. Its coming-of-age theme at "a moment of danger" embodies the common impetus among many filmmakers of the New Hong Kong Cinema to narrate their stories of growing up. Chan's passionate engagement with Hong Kong as a locality adds an indispensable dimension to this tale of disenchanted youth.

When it emerged in 1997, *Made in Hong Kong* was initially denied formal entry into the Hong Kong International Film Festival. With the help of distributors like Shu Kei and Daniel Yu Wai-kwok, it was later screened in Hong Kong and circulated in many international festivals. The film then went on to win numerous awards, including Locarno's Special Jury Prize (Switzerland), Gijon's Grand Prix (Spain), Nantes's Grand Prix (France), and Best Film and Best Director at the Hong Kong Film Awards. It signals an important turn in the history of Hong Kong cinema and in Chan's own career, as a landmark of "independent filmmaking." There is no doubt that alternative and experimental filmmaking had existed in Hong Kong for a long time before the emergence of *Made in Hong Kong*. Nevertheless, Chan's own forthright assertion of the film as an "independent" production inspired a number of similar endeavors in that direction.[8] The revival in independent filmmaking in the late 1990s in Hong Kong was also in constant interaction with the so-called Sixth/Urban Generation of filmmakers in the People's Republic of China. Some critics suggest that Chan shifted back to the mainstream with *Hollywood Hong Kong* (2001) and *Dumplings* (2004), but it is not an uncommon practice for filmmakers to have parallel developments in both mainstream and independent filmmaking. His short film named *Xi'an Story* (2006) was sponsored by a mainland Chinese media company with the aim of providing entertainment for mobile-phone users. It has never been available in Hong Kong commercial cinemas and was only circulated through the international festival circuit.[9]

Chan's constant cross-over between the mainstream and the independent cinemas has sparked public discussions concerning the relation between cinema and its publics. Analyzing his explosive independent debut of *Made in Hong Kong*, we can explore how cinema functions as a form of public criticism. Apart from being both art and industry, cinema is defined by specific relations of representation and reception in what Miriam Hansen calls the "social horizon of experience" grounded in "the context of living."[10] While the title of the film undoubtedly connotes a sense of place which is most local, the cultural issues it evokes are best understood within the context of globalization.[11] The interest lies in the film's double-coded meaning of the specific and the universal, and the ways in which it was received and circulated across geo-political boundaries. Observation of the global-local connection textually and contextually provides us with greater understanding of the deterritorialized structures of public life in our contemporary world. In such instances, we can witness the pressure of the grassroots and the insertion of personal meaning by social actors in the vast, fluid, and anonymous global space of flows. In this process of what Manuel Castells would call "the grassrooting [of] the space of flows," Chan's cinematic practices enrich our public culture by his constant efforts to bring about the contestation of public opinion.[12]

Made in Hong Kong and New Hong Kong Cinema

The making of the film

On various occasions, Chan claimed that the film was made to launch a revolution. He spoke with revolutionary rhetoric as a filmmaker who had worked in the film industry for more than ten years. Chan was born in Guangzhou, China in 1959, and moved to Hong Kong at the age of ten. Chan studied filmmaking at the Hong Kong Film Culture Centre set up by Tsui Hark, Ann Hui, Yim Ho, and others, and worked as an assistant director in the industry for many years. Before his independent debut, he had the opportunity to make two mainstream features. While *Finale in Blood* (produced in 1991 and released in 1993) turned out to be a box-office failure, *Five Lonely Hearts* (1991) has never been screened in Hong Kong. In the mid-1990s when the Hong Kong film industry sank into a slump, Chan was frustrated by his inability to get industrial sponsorship for his film. He then decided to go "independent" to make a film of immense significance at a historical moment of transition. Chan said that the film was intended to be revolutionary in both the context of Hong Kong history and its film history:

> I wanted to revolutionize my life. I had been working in the mainstream industry for a long time, but if I had continued conforming to its norms, I wouldn't have shot *Made in Hong Kong*. Suddenly making an independent production is a revolution for each and every filmmaker in the mainstream. Moreover, the content of independent films usually subverts institutions and that's revolutionary to me as well.[13]

The making of *Made in Hong Kong* does have a legendary story to tell. Throughout his years of toiling in the industry, he raised about half a million Hong Kong dollars and relied on a crew of only five people to accomplish his production.[14] With Lam Wah-chuen and O Sing-pui as cinematographers, Chan directed and scripted the film. Li Tung-chuen, the script supervisor, also played Sylvester in the film. As a team, they insisted on pursuing the greatest degree of independence and freedom without working for any industrial investors. With superstar Andy Lau's generous support, they were able to save up 80,000 feet of short ends of films from Team Work Production House and other sources. According to cinematographer O Sing-pui, many of the film stocks had expired for more than seven years. Lau also agreed to be their executive producer and helped them in the distribution process. Because of the small budget, Chan cast non-professionals whom he found in the street.

When Chan scouted him, Sam Lee, the male protagonist, was literally a boy in the street playing with a skateboard. Other actresses such as Neiky Yim and Amy Tam were first-timers on the big screen. In addition to the financial constraints, Chan had a strong belief in the authentic appeal that amateur actors can deliver. He later made films such as *Little Cheung* (1999) and *Durian Durian* (2000), casting many non-professional actors who "simply act out their own lives."[15] After this initial success, Chan made himself well known through the local and international art-house festival circuit and received funding from overseas sources for his later films.[16] *Made in Hong Kong* would become the first film in Chan's "Handover Trilogy," followed by *The Longest Summer* (1998) and *Little Cheung*. His second incomplete trio called "Trilogy of the Prostitute" consists of *Durian Durian* and *Hollywood Hong Kong*. More recently he made *Public Toilet* (2002), *Dumplings*, and *Xi'an Story*.[17]

Between art and industry

Some critics describe independent cinema as an alternative entity in opposition to mainstream, industrial cinema.[18] Hong Kong independent cinema, however, cannot be understood as a totality or in simple, unified opposition to the mainstream. "Independent" is indeed a sufficiently flexible term embracing a variety of ideological or stylistic expressions. Chan's case offers a precious opportunity to come to grips with the multifarious patterns of independent filmmaking, challenging our understanding of what it means to be "independent" or "mainstream." This is a central question in Chapter 2, where different patterns of independent filmmaking in Hong Kong are examined.

Despite his independent oeuvres, *Made in Hong Kong* does not exhibit all of the typical characteristics of art cinema. On the one hand, the film embodies strong authorial expressivity and realism that is often associated with art or alternative cinema. On the other hand, the film qualifies as a typical Hong Kong genre film.

The intention that Chan and his crew adhered to in the process of making the film asserts that it is a work of art of an expressive individual. Celebrating the notion of *politique des auteurs*, Chan does not shy away from this romantic view of auteurism:[19]

> It's like some spiritual forces pushing me to make this film. I just felt that the timing was right and it was my turn. I had turned down many jobs, because I felt a great passion to finish the film — I knew I had to seize the moment — I didn't care about making money.[20]

This kind of self-positioning as an expressive auteur, intertwined with the sense of urgency to pursue what is timely and non-commercial, suggests that "indies" often define themselves in association with moral notions such as authenticity and social responsibility. In terms of style and aesthetic, these notions govern the emphasis on realism in some independent and art films. However, the common association with realism has in fact been a bone of contention between Chan and his critics. While critics often describe his films as "realistic" and some place him in the tradition of social realism in Hong Kong cinema,[21] Chan constantly prefers to emphasize the creative treatment in his realist films. Despite its affinity to art cinema and its "independent" mode of production, *Made in Hong Kong* is a genre piece of an impure kind. In terms of style and generic conventions, it is quite a typical Hong Kong film of the gangster genre or of youth film with some melodramatic and surrealistic elements. Film critic Tony Rayns is right to point out that the film cannot be simply understood as a typical kind of independent experimentation:

In short, Chan's film was the first Hong Kong feature which could be called an "indie" in the sense that the Sundance Festival once meant it, but the film is smart and accomplished enough to deserve better than to be treated as an enterprising novelty. Chan's background in the industry inflects it at every level. It's at once an insider's attempt to unlearn some bad industry habits, a professional's bid to beat commercial rivals at their own game, and an outsider's criticism of the ways the industry has glamorised the current generation of juvenile delinquents. Another independent director coming to this project without Chan's history behind him certainly would have made a very different film.[22]

I agree with Rayns that the film is a combination of the insider's professional finesse and the outsider's critical stance. The glamorization of the "current juvenile delinquents" that he talks about can be found in Chan's critical views of the naïve heroism in Andrew Lau's *Young and Dangerous* series (1996–2000). If the film can be described as "a legend of Hong Kong independent cinema," I would argue that the two terrains of the independent and the mainstream do not exist in isolation from each other. They in fact influence each other thematically and stylistically. Chan's film style adhered less and less to popular genre (i.e. the gangster genre in particular) after *Made in Hong Kong* and *The Longest Summer*. The mode of social realism and semi-documentary realism in *Little Cheung* and *Durian Durian* brought him closer and closer to the aesthetic style of "art-house" films. However, the generic nature of *Made in Hong Kong* offers an alternative view of seeing Hong Kong's problem youth at a critical moment of transition.[23]

When Ackbar Abbas assesses the New Hong Kong Cinema, he describes the filmmakers as occupying an in-between space between art and commerce. They demonstrate what he calls a "critical proximity," which means that Hong Kong filmmakers who are working in the industry maintain an "intimate" but "critical" relationship with the commercial film culture in which they are situated. Examples of this group are Wong Kar-wai, Stanley Kwan, and Ann Hui. Abbas claims that such cinematic movements always begin with a specific film genre only to deviate from the generic convention quite radically. The deviation points punctually to changing circumstances which are expressed in new forms. Their films thus exemplify some common traits of the "New Hong Kong Cinema": "its adoption of spatial narratives to suggest dislocations, a new complexity in the treatment of affects and emotions, a creative use of popular genres, a new localism, and a politics that can only be indirect."[24]

From the production history of *Made in Hong Kong* outlined above, we can see an example of "in-betweenness" within this kind of "in-betweenness." Chan is more ambiguous than his cohorts in the New Hong Kong Cinema. On the one hand, having worked in the industry for many years, he acted like a self-styled filmmaker who willfully chose to disentangle himself from it at a critical historical moment. His forthright declaration of making the film with a mission and his pursuit of the independent mode of filmmaking between 1997 and 2002 place him safely in the terrain of the "independent" cinema. Even more recently when he declared a return to the mainstream again, he constantly utilized his "otherness" and oppositionality to launch a cultural politics which is in no way indirect. He gladly accepts the label as a "grassroots director."[25] On the other hand, despite his intentional distancing from the mainstream, in terms of funding sources, his independent debut cannot be considered as totally separable from the mainstream because he did receive some resources from Andy Lau's Team Work. Strictly speaking, instead of absolute autonomy, his auteurism bears traces of the form of intersubjectivity described by Timothy Corrigan.[26] In terms of style and generic conventions, he exercises a similar kind of "critical proximity" shared by the Hong Kong filmmakers mentioned earlier. Thematically he shares with Stanley Kwan and Wong Kar-wai the concern for articulating the cultural experience of space-time dislocation caused by tumultuous historical change and the incessant processes of globalization. In the global circulation and reception of the so-called "Hong Kong art-house," these three filmmakers represent a strand of Hong Kong cinema which is alternative to the action genre popularized by Jackie Chan and John Woo, among many others.[27] While Fruit Chan can be placed alongside Kwan and Wong, one idiosyncratic feature that distinguishes him from the other two is his persistence in the depiction of the cultural experience and psychological condition of the people from the lowest socio-economic class. In this regard, he shares with Ann Hui and Allen Fong a concern for the plight of the ordinary people. He is also comparable to Lawrence Lau (aka Lawrence Ah Mon) and Herman Yau, who have portrayed problem youth and marginalized existences. Beyond Hong Kong cinema, one may also connect Chan with a great many filmmakers in Chinese-language cinemas such as Edward Yang from Taiwan and Zhang Yuan and Jia Zhangke from the PRC, as well as earlier classics by Nagisa Oshima in the international film scene.[28] When Law Kar analyzes the First Wave filmmakers of Hong Kong cinema, he sees them as part of the global activist and counter-culture movement in the 1960s and 70s.[29] Younger than the First Wavers, Chan shares with them an acute social consciousness in the realist tradition of local and global film cultures.

In retrospect, *Made in Hong Kong* was clearly a wellspring of Chan's later film productions because it set off a series of persistent attempts in a similar direction. Despite the different emphases in his various films, Chan is determined to re-create the city of Hong Kong as an ambiguous, abject space that has not been "whitewashed by detergent," as one film critic puts it.[30] This space is also filled with abject characters — gangsters and forgotten youth (*Made in Hong Kong* and *The Longest Summer*), prostitutes (*Durian Durian* and *Hollywood Hong Kong*), and illegal immigrants (*Little Cheung* and *Durian Durian*) — all forming an array of human images whose social and cultural marginality have paradoxically occupied a symbolically central position in Chan's films. In contrast to the glamorous touristic Victoria skyline, the city spaces in his films are found in the derelict public housing estates in Kwai Chung, Kwun Tong, Tuen Mun, and Sha Tin, dirty back-alleys in Mong Kok and Yau Ma Tei, the now-demolished slum Tai Hom Village, and many more.

Critical literature on the film

Made in Hong Kong bears many credentials as a film of the New Hong Kong Cinema. Critics are generally interested in elucidating the double bind of generality and specificity argued earlier. Two interrelated strands of critical views, among others, have shaped interpretations of the film. In the first instance, the film is read in the context of class and social marginality. In her critical essay "The Cruel Tragedy of Youth: On Fruit Chan's *Made in Hong Kong*," Natalia Chan Sui-hung points out that the themes of youth and death are central to the film. The miracle of the film lies in its "perception that exhibits the world of Hong Kong's youth with deep sympathy and understanding."[31] By illuminating a living space closely associated with the lower-class inhabitants of Hong Kong, the film "depicts the life and inner world of youth who strive to survive in the social margin."[32] In light of Michel Foucault's concept of "heterotopias" (literally meaning "other spaces"), she explores the relationship between various spaces in the film and the marginal culture of youth in Hong Kong. The film reveals that Hong Kong is "a society without a father," which metaphorically is "related to Hong Kong's political situation, especially in light of its handover in 1997."[33] Sharing Chan's view on class and marginality, Wimal Dissanayake attributes Moon's alienated sentiments about the rapidly changing world and the decline of the family to "the intrusiveness of capitalist modernity." In "The Class Imaginary in Fruit Chan's Films," he suggests that Chan's work "allows us to focus on class as an important concept in understanding the filmic representations of social experience."[34]

To connect this general notion of class and marginality to Hong Kong's historical context, Yau Ka-fai uses *Made in Hong Kong* and the other two parts of the "Handover Trilogy" to explore his concept of a "minor Hong Kong cinema" as "a cinema that deterritorializes within the heart of what is considered major."[35] It is less "a cinema at the margin" than "a strategy to conceptualize and develop certain suggestive examples in order to respond to specific geo-historical situations." Yau claims that the "Handover Trilogy" dwells upon "the failed, the vanished, and the under-represented to make Hong Kong appear at the intriguing moment of 1997, as well as explore new perspectives for re-channeling Hong Kong and its histories."[36]

Laikwan Pang takes the theme of death a step further to explore the film in the context of Hong Kong's cultural identity. In "Death and Hong Kong Cinema," she suggests that the confused state of the four youngsters' identities forces the audience to reflect on the meaning of their deaths:

> Instead, they are trapped in the threshold between youth and adulthood, and their deaths can be seen as a willful challenge and refusal to pass through the rite of passage provided by the institution in order to remain infinitely in the enjoyment of "non-identity."[37]

To her, Susan's dead letter to her parents "establishes a communication between the two generations, between the deceased and her parents." Moon's posthumous voice throughout the film also makes connection with the audience directly. Although there is a sense of uncertainty about Hong Kong's identity at a moment of critical transition, the film suggests that "its subjectivity is clearly revealed in the very process of communication." Dialogue is possible beyond and after the youngsters' death trips:

> Death crystallizes the communication difficulties between the two generations, and allegorically between the two lands of Hong Kong and the mainland; but at the same time it also makes dialogue possible.[38]

Shu-mei Shih, in her "After National Allegory," also reads *Made in Hong Kong* as an allegorical narrative. She analyzes the "national" allegorical implications in Chan's "Handover Trilogy" to illustrate the subtle changes in Hong Kong's sense of identity in relation to its colonial past and Chinese rule after the handover. She suggests that the allegorical subject in *Made in Hong Kong*, the first part of the "Handover Trilogy," is time itself:

> It is about the negation of colonial-inflected temporality of nostalgia and Chinese temporality of history ("the future belongs to China"), and the displacement of these temporalities by a different one that exceeds and escapes definition in normative language. Through this temporality, an ambiguous sense of Hong Kong cultural identity is articulated in the form of double refusal: refusing the temporality of colonial nostalgia as well as Chinese takeover.[39]

While these interpretations touch on the double-coded meaning of the general and the specific, many issues still remain to be examined. How do we understand Chan's realism in relation to his independent motivations? What kinds of aesthetic and cultural values are disseminated in independent oeuvres like Chan's? How do we decipher class and social marginality in relation to Hong Kong's specific architectural and living spaces? In what way can the assertion of subjectivity be revealed through the analysis of the ghostly afterlife beyond death? How do the film's *mise-en-scène*, sound and voice, camera shots as well as narrative structure shape our understanding of the double bind? The close readings of the film in subsequent chapters attempt to tackle these intriguing questions.

Reading the film: angle, method, and approach

Made in Hong Kong shows a carefully crafted web-of-life plotline which weaves together four major lines of action. This is a common narrative technique in classic and contemporary youth films in world cinema. Precedents of these in international cinema can be found in Luis Buñuel's *The Forgotten Ones* (*Los Olvidados*, 1950) and Oshima's *Cruel Tragedy of Youth* (*Seishun zankoku monogatari*, 1960). More recent productions in Chinese-language cinemas, such as Zhang Yuan's *Beijing Bastards* (1993) and Tsai Ming-liang's *Rebels of the Neon God* (1992), also involve many disenchanted youthful characters and the ways in which their paths intersect. Like these youth films about urban alienation, each major character in *Made in Hong Kong* functions to illuminate some basic problems of capitalistic modernity. Themes of marginality, alienation, homelessness, and death are central to the critique of such a society. Despite this grim portrayal, Chan holds on to a simple faith in the potential for genuine human communion among the youngsters themselves. Such a communion may be short-lived and rare but it serves well as an act of "disalienation" that counters the condition of estrangement.

The film begins with two important segments which introduce the four major characters. The opening scene is a group of youngsters playing in a basketball court, in which Moon's voice-over narrates his and Sylvester's background as lower-class inhabitants in the government housing estates. Like many ordinary teenage boys who find the basketball playground more spacious than their congested cubicles, they figure as disaffected kids at the margin of Hong Kong society. Moon works for triad gangs and identifies himself as a "young gangster." He boasts ironically that he has a mentally retarded boy, Sylvester, as his follower. In the same segment, Moon and Sylvester meet Ping and her mother in another type of public housing estate, suggesting that Ping shares a similar lower-class background. This is followed by a segment on Susan's suicide after her lonesome stroll on the rooftop of a building. It is a major scene shot in light blue tone which recurs in the latter parts of the film. Sylvester then picks up Susan's two dead letters which later are in Moon's hands.

While the film provides an intricate web of the youngsters' lives, Moon's point of view is the major focus. His voice-over not only serves as a narrative device throughout the whole film but also functions as an eerie dead man's voice, or what Michel Chion calls an *acousmêtre*. It takes us through a series of death trips with Moon's commentary on an earlier state of himself, his peers, and the society in which he lives.

Moon lives in a broken family where he is in constant conflict with his mother about his father's extra-marital affair and problems about family expenses. Abandoning the family, his father keeps a mistress and a baby girl. As a high school drop-out, Moon becomes his mother's object of scorn. While he admires and imitates heroes of action films in both local and international cinemas, he lacks any heroic stature and offers no hope and future from his mother's point of view. Tired of such a shattered situation, his mother also shirks her parental responsibility and runs away. Moon does not have a proper job, leading a wretched life by collecting debts for triad gangsters. During this meaningless business, he meets Ping and flirts with her. Witnessing Ping in a similarly unhappy family and suffering from a terminal disease, Moon wishes to save her but in vain. With a pistol from Brother Wing, one gangster leader, he also fails to carry out an assassination assignment of murdering two businessmen from Shenzhen. After this failed mission, he is attacked by an unknown gangster and then hospitalized. He survives the murder only to be informed of Ping's death. As Sylvester is proved useless to the gangster, he is then tragically gunned to death. Knowing this sad news, Moon decides to shoot Brother Wing. As a successful avenger of his friend's death, he is finally exiled on a path of no return. After killing Brother Wing and another gangster Fat Chan, he commits suicide, following in Susan's footsteps. He ends his journey of death right before the Hong Kong handover in 1997. In his ghostly acousmatic voice, he narrates the last scene of the film where he has a spiritual communion with Ping, Sylvester, and Susan.

The symbolic meanings of Moon depend largely on the roles and functions of the two primary female characters and Sylvester. Like Moon, Ping grows up in a fatherless family. Being abandoned, she and her mother are continuously harassed by loan sharks and triad gangs. With her fatal kidney disease, she hopelessly awaits her impending death. Unlike Moon who motivates his own actions, Ping is more passive and has no control over her life. Even the issue of her kidney transplant is communicated between her mother and the social worker. Her destiny is in the hands of failing adults who do not have the ability to protect her. She flirts with Moon and enjoys being with him and Sylvester. They spend their time together in congested housing estates and in the graveyard. Toward the end, Moon moans over the brevity of her life and laments that he could not save her. In a similar way, Susan embarks on a short and tragic journey. She is also portrayed as a lower-class inhabitant as her aged parents reside in a public housing estate. The depiction of her unfortunate romantic relationship with her teacher is brief but serves well to parallel the experiences of abandonment shared by the other youngsters. She remains a voiceless apparition who appears in Moon's wet dreams and fantasies until the very end of the film when she reads aloud her own dead letter. She figures as an image rather than a fully developed character. Her victimhood illuminates the disaffection of other youngsters, especially Sylvester who is constantly subject to other people's maltreatment because he is mentally retarded. Again and again, he is bullied by teenage schoolboys in the street and in the public toilet. While he is the one who picks up Susan's dead letters, he does not have a clear idea of the message of death. However, he is not immune from death and suffering. Like Ping, he does not have control over his life. He follows Moon around, hopelessly seeking protection which can only be temporary. He is killed by triads when he is no longer instrumental. A moving, albeit inarticulate and unheroic character, he shares all the other youngsters' longing for care and concern in a heartless city. He expresses his innocent yearning for communion through his crush on Ping and his genuine friendship with Moon.

The most interesting things about the film cannot be recapitulated precisely and thoroughly by the plot summaries and character sketches above. To show how the bleak destinies of the youngsters are intertwined with each other, Chan develops a film narrative with a unified set of interdependent elements which include color, sound, voice, characterization, and camera shots and movements. The recurrent motifs of death, such as suicide, terminal disease, dark indoor spaces, graveyard, hospital, and murder, unravel an ensemble of death voyages. The repeated use of major scenes and images which provide parallelism and echoes of rhythm contributes to the poetic power of the film. The artistic employment of parametric elements such as sound and voice-over are central to understanding the possibility of communication in the ghostly afterlife of the characters. The later chapters of this book demonstrate how these film elements illuminate the themes of youth, death, marginality, and alienation.

There exists a variety of methods to reading films, including film-formalistic analysis, theory-driven approaches informed by Marxism, psychoanalysis, feminism, semiology, and more recent cultural studies approaches. This book offers some historical, cultural, and theoretical perspectives to the reading of Chan's remarkable film, emphasizing the importance of textual studies and strategies of reading the film images of death and marginality in their historical and cultural contexts. Instead of adopting a segment-by-segment analysis, it is organized through major arguments and topics pertaining to the social and cultural milieu of Hong Kong and the rest of the world. This approach also stresses the need to decipher the history of a given film's production, distribution, and reception, exploring related issues of authorial intention, intersubjectivity, and imagined communities.

While emphasizing *Made in Hong Kong*, the book sheds comparative light on Chan's later work and other categories of Hong Kong and global cinema. While genre classification is never neat and stable, *Made in Hong Kong* is discussed in relation to genres such as ghost, gangster, and martial arts films as well as stories about problem youth and growing up. To interrogate the notion of "independence," Chapter 2 discusses the problem of periodization and classification of independent films in Hong Kong, and illustrates how Chan's "independent motivations and intentions" have shaped the politics of access and recognition that he plays out in his cinematic practices. It foregrounds the ways in which aesthetic and cultural values are disseminated and circulated in a deterritorialized global space.

What follows are two chapters to be read in conjunction with each other. Chapter 3 explores Chan's "impure" realistic film style in Hong Kong's specific cinematic context and in comparison with other filmmakers in world cinema and contemporary Chinese-language cinema. Chapter 4 shows that genre subversion in *Made in Hong Kong* is done with the mobilization of "realistic" elements as an effective means of defamiliarization. My argument is that "realistic motivations," as neo-formalists would call them, do not only aim to "reflect" but also to "defamiliarize" the "real." I call this endeavor, following Guy Debord, an "art of *détournement*" to indicate that artistic recoding of the heroic young gangster genre in *Made in Hong Kong* is both a strategy of resistance and an articulation of voices from the grassroots. Realism as a style is then a form of social and cultural critique.

Chapters 5 and 6 continue with this issue of marginality in the socio-economic dimension by focusing on Chan's "quasi-realism," which refers to his mixed use of surrealistic and ghostly elements in his "social-realist" films. Through the conceptualization of the "ghostly city" as an aesthetic category in his films, haunting as an epistemology serves as an antidote to mystification. While the study of aesthetics may entail what is universal and generalizing, the feeling of homelssness is contextualized in the history of Hong Kong's low-cost housing estates and other similar marginalized urban spaces. This historicized view of "the ghostly" in what is local, grassroots, and unique in Hong Kong cannot be understood without reference to how the homogenizing and hegemonic forces are suppressing and repressing the histories of forgotten people and spaces. This observation of the local-global connection offers different views to understanding the film as an epitome of localism. Chapter 6 in particular is primarily concerned with how this demystification of "the ghostly" provides access to the "secrets of class" inherent in the haunting feeling. It analyzes how "the ghostly" generates possibilities of countering estrangement and alienation at the levels of representation and reception, and asks how we can speak about personal expression and purposeful horizontal communication in a world of many constraints. While admitting the limitations of the Romantic notion of "the personal," it is enlightening to see how "the personal" offers ways of surviving in an intersubjective web of socio-economic relations.

2

Authenticity and Independence:
Fruit Chan and Independent Filmmaking

Freedom exists and is limited, such as birth place and time.

— Jean-Paul Sartre[1]

The problem of classification: a historical perspective

Independent and experimental filmmaking has existed for many decades. However, as independent filmmaker Bryan Chang claims, there has never been such a film movement in Hong Kong, no matter how politically conscious and cosmopolitan its filmmakers have been.[2] In their slightly different periodizations of Hong Kong independent cinema, both May Fung, a veteran video-artist in Hong Kong, and Connie Lam trace its beginning to the 1960s, emphasizing the importance of the 1990s revival.[3]

To quote from Lam, the 1960s was an exciting time when Super 8 and 16mm films were introduced to Hong Kong, paving the way for developments in the 1970s when cine clubs and annual competitions were held to celebrate and support independent filmmaking. Before the 1980s when the government's subsidies for cinema activities were relatively limited, civil cine clubs played an important role in promoting an "alternative" film culture among local film lovers. Set up in 1962, Studio One was the first of its kind in Hong Kong. The organizers of Studio One were largely expatriates in Hong Kong. Since then cine club activities have been popular among college and university students, who also organized their own cine clubs. In 1967, editors and writers from youth cultural periodicals formed College Cine Club. Many core members of the club later became important figures in cultural fields and the cinema industry. For instance, film director Ho Fan, scriptwriter and critic Kam Ping-hing, film director and critic Lau Shing-hon, film historian and scriptwriter Lin Lien-tung, film critics Law Kar and Sek Kei, and writer Xi Xi were members of the group. Regular activities of these clubs included film shows, seminars, experimental film exhibitions, and short filmmaking. The films that they screened were largely those by auteurs and masters from Europe, the USA, and Japan. The experimental films that they showed were mostly made by their members, thus encouraged more young people to engage in amateur filmmaking. Between 1966 and 1970, about fifty experimental short films were made.[4]

College Cine Club closed in 1971, but Film Guard Association and Phoenix Cine Club were set up in 1971 and 1973 respectively with the same objectives. They continued to organize experimental film exhibitions, with sponsorship from the Urban Council. The Hong Kong International Film Festival, inaugurated in 1977, was organized by the Urban Council with co-operation from Phoenix Cine Club and Film Guard. In 1978, the Film Culture Centre of Hong Kong was founded by a group of up-and-coming figures in television. It offered production courses and also functioned as a film club. From the mid-1970s to early 80s, Phoenix Cine Club also co-organized Hong Kong Independent Short Film Exhibition regularly with the Urban Council. The 1970s saw a flourishing era of work in Super 8. An estimated two hundred pieces of work were made by a hundred amateur film practitioners.[5] Emerging from these film exhibitions were Neco Lo, a significant figure in Hong Kong independent filmmaking for animation since the mid-1970s, and Lawrence Lau, Alex Cheung, as well as Eddie Fong who later entered the cinema industry and became recognizable figures of the Hong Kong New Wave. After Phoenix Cine Club was closed in 1987, some of its members formed Videotage with the objective to promote video and new media art.

After the relatively quiet late 1980s, the 1990s witnessed a revival as the newly created Hong Kong Arts Development Council (ADC) boosted the development of independent cinema. According to Lam, 1993 can be regarded as the comeback year of Hong Kong's independent productions because the Hong Kong Independent Shorts Film Competition was revived and at the same time, the Hong Kong Arts Centre received funding to organize the first Hong Kong Independent Video Awards and to improve the facilities for filmmaking. Most notably in 1995, the Urban Council, which was renamed Leisure and Cultural Services Department in 2000, collaborated with Arts Centre to launch the Hong Kong Independent Short Films and Video Awards (IFVA) as an annual event. Between 1996 and 2000, unprecedented government sponsorship was provided for independent filmmaking, encouraging a total of thirty-three film projects.[6] In a broader socio-political context, the 1990s was also a time when the mainstream industry was declining and Hong Kong society was undergoing its critical transition to the 1997 handover.

Undeniably, the ways that film history is periodized reflect the criteria that critics use to define what "independent" means. In a project titled *i-Generations: Independent, Experimental and Alternative Creations from the 60s to Now* conducted in 2001,

May Fung outlines the development of Hong Kong independent productions in a similar way, paying specific attention to how different periods are characterized by different technological changes. From the use of 16mm and Super 8 in the 1960s and 70s to the more current use of video and digital camera in the new millennium, Fung observes an intimate relationship between technology and creativity. She also notices that while there has been a persistent trend of experimental filmmaking in Hong Kong film history, the earlier indies were more concerned with experimentation, innovation, and a sense of mission whereas recent ones are more interested in being recognized. To rationalize her periodization, she clearly mentions two criteria which define "independence": any film, which is produced by the filmmakers' own effort to seek funding and which is characterized by fresh perspective, innovative spirit, and personal vision, can be regarded as an independent production. According to her, even if the productions may end up being distributed in the commercial and industrial network, their spirit of autonomy cannot be annihilated.[7] One exemplar is *The Arch* (1969), a film by Tang Shu-shuen who is regarded as one of the first independent filmmakers in Hong Kong. The film was produced by Cathay Studios and Tang's own production house with some support from an American independent film company. Tang had full control as director, scriptwriter, and producer. From some critics' point of view, *The Arch* embraces the independent spirit in many ways: its subject matter, its innovative techniques, its funding, its production, and its screenings in cine clubs.[8]

Fung and Lam offer a standard perspective of understanding Hong Kong independent cinema. Fung's approach, in particular, coincides with the conventional view in Western scholarship: independent films are those that are produced outside the studio systems and with the spirit of autonomy.[9] Various critics, however, have already agreed that this spirit of independence does not necessarily have anything to do with financial independence. The case of the French New Wave in the 1960s can illustrate this idea. As Stuart Klawans et al. suggest, although the French New Wave was a response to the developing conditions of foreign competition and televisual rivalry, its members demanded access to that system.[10] In fact in other cases of national cinema, state funding is the major source; the revival of Hong Kong independent films in the 1990s was a case in point. Greg Merritt raises another point that complicates the definition of the independent cinema. He believes that the spirit of independence upheld by filmmakers can become something marketable; one is not surprised to discover that the biggest independent studios are owned by the biggest media conglomerates.[11] In light of these exceptions, it is right for Chuck Kleinhans to suggest that the concept of "'independence,' then, has to be understood as a relational term — independent in relation to the dominant system — rather than taken as indicating a practice that is totally free-standing and autonomous."[12]

Some, including many independent practitioners themselves, suggest that it is not productive to separate the two. Two proponents in Hong Kong who advocate such a flexible view are Bryan Chang and Vincent Chui. Chang maintains that the development of independent film can never be separated from the mainstream:

> Our market is too small to allow turf demarcation, or we will just have two maimed sides. A self-sufficient operation is the long-term aim of indies, but that does not necessarily mean it has to be exclusive. Indies need to gain the trust of their commercial counterpart in order to be a non-regular side of the movie industry. On the other hand, for a more diversified growth, the movie industry should be more flexible in accepting indies as part of the movie scene.[13]

Vincent Chui, another indie filmmaker who has attempted to traverse the terrains of the "mainstream" and "independent," points out the difficulty of dissociating one from another:

What constitutes an entity? We don't have any rights to vote as a functional constituency! (Laughs) Independent films never have a uniform style, their only difference is a relatively free creative approach as opposed to the mainstream industry. Among the filmmakers, there are some who only want to use indie as a stepping stone to the mainstream through the independent spirit, like Quentin Tarantino. Some have always been true to themselves, making personal experimental works, like Spike Lee. Yet I still feel that only after indie filmmakers have achieved commercial success can the influence of the independent cinema be significant.[14]

Hong Kong indie cinema is indeed characterized by variety, both in terms of modes of production and distribution and the sources of funding. The personal history and background of different Hong Kong independent filmmakers also vary a great deal.[15] In the recent revival of indie cinema in the 1990s, apart from government sponsorship, we can also witness more and more support coming from the commercial sector. Mainstream film producers Eric Tsang and Andrew Wai-keung Lau as well as superstar Andy Lau, in their different ways, have been supporting young and independent filmmakers to nurture their creativity in filmmaking. *Made in Hong Kong* is just one pioneering example in this recent trend. Mainstream film companies, in fact, very often invite celebrated filmmakers in the independent sphere to make commercial films, with the aim of attracting a more sophisticated audience. Ann Hui, Stanley Kwan, and Herman Yau are some notable examples in the industry. For some independent filmmakers, making commercial films can be a way to raise funding for their projects and also to stay active in the film industry. It is thus apt to say that this relation between the mainstream and independent is so intimate that they are inseparable from each other.[16]

The above views expressed by Chui can be understood within the context of such interactions. Chui is one of the founders of

Ying E Chi, a non-profit film group established by a number of independent filmmakers in 1997 to promote independent filmmaking and help its distribution in Hong Kong. He initially emerged as an independent film worker in the most conventional sense in the 1990s; however, in later years, he made *Fear of Intimacy* (2004) which shows many signs of the cross-over between the mainstream and the independent. The film was financed by an industrial company, cast professional stars, and adopted the form of a commercial genre film. Around the same time, Carol Lai's *The Floating Landscape* (2003), Edmond Pang's *Men Suddenly in Black* (2003), Wong Ching-po's *Jiang Hu* (2004), and Yan Yan Mak's *Butterfly* (2004) were made in the same pattern. Among these young independent filmmakers, Pang has gotten a strong footing in a relatively short period of time. He made his first short DV, *Summer Exercise*, in 1999 which won an award at the IFVA, and within two years he got financial resources from Golden Harvest for his first feature *You Shoot, I Shoot* (2001), a black comedy with an intent to subvert the stereotypes in traditional Hong Kong killer films. Two years later, his second feature *Men Suddenly in Black*, with a casting of famous artists, won him the Best New Director at the Hong Kong Film Awards. In 2006, his *Isabella* (2006) entered the Berlinale's competition and took home the Silver Bear for Best Film Music (Peter Kam). The works of these young filmmakers all form a more hybrid corpus of indie films entering the mainstream.

In her book on Chan's *Durian Durian*, Wendy Gan identifies two main patterns of independent filmmaking in Hong Kong.[17] The first is experimental in nature, and intimately associated with video art, short film, and documentaries; its production and distribution modes are more detached from the industrial ones. This group is close to the corpus of films that Fung includes in her periodization. Some persistent representatives include Ellen Pau, Yau Ching, Julian Lee, and Anson Mak. The second type is more closely linked with the industry. Gan is perceptive to point out that with the eventual fragmentation of the studio system monopolized by Shaw Brothers since the mid-1970s, there emerged independent film companies which provided opportunities for film workers. Quite a number of industrial directors from the New Wave Cinema, for example, Allen Fong and Yim Ho, belong to this category. More recently many others such as Fruit Chan, Stanley Kwan, Herman Yau, Nelson Yu Lik-wai, and even Wong Kar-wai have come out of this same "'independent' commercial industry."[18] It is also because of this group's in-between status that Fung and Lam have not considered them at length in their classification and periodization. Gan even calls this group the "Hong Kong–style" independent filmmaking. This broader definition of independent cinema illuminates our understanding of the dynamic processes of interaction between the mainstream and the independent spheres. Nevertheless, it should be noted that some may not compromise with this "Hong Kong–style" independent filmmaking. Clara Law stated in an interview that she and her partner Eddie Fong would never be part of the Hong Kong mainstream, which was too commercial and entertainment-oriented. The principal reason for their relocation to Australia (around 1994–95) was to seek more support, greater independence, and creative space.[19] In recent years, local independent filmmakers have often set up a production company of their own in order to gain more control of the production process and enable them to seek funding from various sources at home and abroad. When the local film industry is in a downturn, they seek adequate resources through different means.

Interrogating "independence"

This in-betweenness can be traced back to the Hong Kong New Wave in the early 1980s. However, the meaning of independence has never been clearly addressed in the film discourse. From an existentialist point of view, while there is no absolute freedom in this world but only freedom within constraints, the same can be said about the pursuit of independence within the commercial industry. The system is not a form of total domination but subject to ongoing processes of hegemonic negotiations, as the followers of Raymond Williams and the critics of the Frankfurt School would argue.[20] While this view is salient and convincing, there are two sets of unresolved questions. First, what exactly does "independence" mean? Since "independence" is often invoked in association with tropes such as "authenticity" (or sometimes phrased as "being true to oneself"), "creative freedom," "personal vision," "authorial expressivity," and so on, it suggests that independence could mean many things. When "independence" is deciphered as an "attitude" or "spirit" which cannot evoke fixed meanings, especially when one can urge for "independence" within the mainstream, "independence" becomes a qualifier whose meaning can only be fixed in relation to something else and must be deciphered in specific contexts.

Secondly, if the two terrains are not easily and productively separable, why is the notion of independence always invoked by film practitioners even when they attempt to find a compromising space within the industry? This is especially obvious with artists like Chan who intentionally foster an oppositional stance and an identity of otherness from industrial filmmaking. Quite a number of Hong Kong indies only strategically use the independent cinema as either a useful label for getting funding from the ADC or a kind of stepping stone to the industry, as Chui remarked.[21] Furthermore, as Chui and others constantly remind us, it is difficult to clearly and safely demarcate a zone called "the independent cinema." While it is true that indies have no unified style, do specific choices of style and subject matter posit an "implied audience" if there is a motivation to be critical and independent? Do such claims of independence help to draw like-minded individuals together to construct imagined communities of their own? The revival in the 1990s and Chan's interesting case provide some answers to these questions.

Fruit Chan's independent oeuvres and cultural values

In Chan's various attempts to traverse between the mainstream and the alternative, one can see the contingent meaning of independence tied with a specific moment of crisis. As mentioned earlier, the making of *Made in Hong Kong* was the result of his decision to "go independent" after many years of service in the film industry. He even describes this change of alignment as an endeavor to launch a revolution. As an attempt to participate in defining the meaning of Hong Kong's identity and cultural space at a changing moment, this specific independent oeuvre is close to one characteristic associated with what I call "crisis-ridden" cultural texts. Chan's revolutionary rhetoric also reminds one of the Romantic notion of commitment to a specific cause. If crisis can be considered as a point of time of critical reflection, the 1997 handover was a cathartic moment where artistic and cultural expressions were stimulated in response to such a change.[22] The crisis vision that Chan conjures up in his films embodies the traits of independent cinema outlined above. Williams once called cultural expressions which come to grips with new and changing circumstances as "emergent" culture.[23] While it is true that what is emergent is not necessarily oppositional, Chan's crisis vision is punctual and critical. This critical engagement with the immediate socio-cultural circumstances, according to Chan, was only possible as a result of pursuit of independence within the industry. This assertion is close to the notion of the "art cinema" where the filmmaker-artist exercises a high degree of control over the filmmaking process and the film can be viewed as a form of personal expression. So "independence" is actualized in the spirits of counter-hegemony and oppositionality.

Chan's personal vision and authorial expressivity are notable in *Made in Hong Kong*, when autobiographical references are made with regard to the experience of growing up in Hong Kong's low-cost government housing. *Little Cheung* shows even more autobiographical references as Chan has said that the film is really a story of his growing up.[24] These kinds of personal references shape an oppositional stance which can be understood in a broader socio-cultural context. Without completely identifying with his characters, Chan is preoccupied with the depiction of marginalized people and unglamorous spaces. If the cultural representations of Hong Kong's success story are celebrations of the privileged, Chan's stories of the marginalized offer us an alternative perspective of understanding Hong Kong's forgotten history through images of otherness. Such images echo the ways he positions independent filmmaking as an entity of otherness from the industrial one. In both *Made in Hong Kong* and *The Longest Summer*, Chan has not resorted to independent shorts or highly experimental films but chosen to produce a genre piece so as to subvert the generic conventions of commercial gangster films. Similar "independent" attempts, though stylistically different from Chan's, are numerous. In "Independent Meditations," Chang observes that in the 1990s when independent cinema was revived by changing political circumstances and enhanced government sponsorship, there were many productions which aimed to tell diverse tales of growing up in Hong Kong.[25] From autobiographical documentaries by more well-known filmmakers such as Ann Hui's *As Time Goes By* (1997) and Stanley Kwan's *Still Love You After All These* (1997) to shorter films like *Father's Toy* (1998) by Carol Lai and *Dreamtrips* (1999) by Kal Ng, one can witness a shared sense of urgency to define identity through the experience of growing up in Hong Kong.

Chan is more explicit in voicing his desire to mobilize the notion of independence to create alternative space within the mainstream. If commitment is a form of alignment which can be regarded as a conscious, active, and open choice of position, this early phase of Chan's filmmaking demonstrates a conscious change of alignment in film practice. Attempts were made to cope with some of the constraints imposed by the commercial and industrial mode of production. Some of these constraints, for example, expensive and glamorous casting, costly technology-intensive special effects, and adherence to generic conventions so as to guarantee audience attendance, have indeed been translated into acts of transgression. The explicit declarations of the motivation to be independent and oppositional, however flamboyant they may sound to some people, generate identifications among like-minded individuals who spread across geo-cultural boundaries forming what we might call "the imagined communities of the indies." In his analysis of the revival of the independent cinema in the 1990s, Sam Ho argues that Chan has become a "role model" for many filmmakers especially through the festival circuit because he "parlayed his industry experience into a fundraising savvy."[26]

Elsewhere I argue that Chan's film art is a practice of "making-do" because of his status between industrial and art-house cinemas.[27] While it is generally true that Chan adopted an independent filmmaking mode, his in-between status allows him to gain financial assistance from film producers in the mainstream. Take *Durian Durian* as an example, which was made following his enhanced international fame after the "Handover Trilogy." The film was produced by Nicetop Independent and Golden Network, and supported by funding from France. He is not completely separated from the industry as Golden Network distributes not only art films but also those with mainstream appeal. The art-house market can be as profitable as the mainstream in a disenchanted world where art can nonetheless be a commodity. Chan is better understood as an insider in the industry who is determined to beat "his commercial rivals at their own game," to quote Rayns.[28] I have followed Michel de Certeau to call it "the art of making-do," which refers to how one can make do by constructing one's own space within and against the other's space, speaking one's own meanings with other people's language.[29] *Durian Durian* did not make impressive box-office records but its artistic value was affirmed by the jury of the Hong Kong Film Awards, which had mainly been paying attention to commercial productions until the emergence of *Made in Hong Kong* in 1997.[30] While it is true that *Durian Durian* adheres less to commercial genres than his earlier films and is more like an art-house production, the film is better known as an alternative at the edge of the mainstream.

Echoes of these values have been found in the ways Chan's independent oeuvres have impacted upon local and international cinematic discourses. After *Made in Hong Kong*, Chan has been circulated in Western and Asian cinematic discourses as an "indie filmmaker." He appeared in a feature on independent filmmaking in indieWIRE, and his films, for example *Little Cheung*, not only attracted the support of Japanese and Korean film groups, but also gained international coverage because of its appearance in many festivals. Some of these outlets include publications such as *Variety, Screen International, El Norte de Castilla, El Correo Vizcaya, La Voz de Asturias*, and *Argus*. In Italy, he was reported in *La Repubblica, La Nuova*, and *Il Gazzettino* due to *Hollywood Hong Kong*'s participation in the Venice Film Festival competition. In Korea, as his influences were increasing after *Public Toilet*, which was financed by Digital NEGA, he appeared very frequently in newspapers and magazines such as *Screen, Daily Munhwa, Cine 21, Nae Way Economic Daily, Movie Week*, and *Nega*. In mainland China, he is termed as a "low-budget" and "grassroots" filmmaker. Even in mainstream Hong Kong tabloids such as *Next Magazine, East Touch*, and *Apple Daily*, he is represented without controversy as an independent filmmaker who suffers from financial constraints.[31] Global cinematic connections have provided Chan opportunities to produce and exhibit his films. In fact, similar to Jia Zhangke and other contemporary Chinese urban filmmakers, he is more well received overseas than locally. Identified now as Hong Kong "art-house" produced and circulated in the space between the global and the local, Chan's films contribute to diversifying the international viewing reception of Asian films, disturbing the tendency toward mono-culturalization or homogenization in global cinematic culture, and providing varieties not only in generic innovation but also in modes of production and distribution.[32]

There are mainly three kinds of values which are asserted in the context of independence: equality, diversity, and authenticity. First, independent filmmaking operates in an industrial space where hierarchies of production exist. In public discourse, Chan's debut is called "the Hong Kong independent legend." His creative use of resources in the industry and his alternative way of gathering funding from friends and international film groups are regarded as ways in which he fights for access to and participatory equity within the commercial institution. He has inspired other indies making low-budget films. Lam Wah-chuen's *The Runaway Pistol* (2002) and Lo Hoi-ying's *Hong Kong Guy* (1998) are quite close in style to *Made in Hong Kong*. Lam, in particular, has been Chan's collaborator in many film projects. He was the cinematographer of *Made in Hong Kong*, *The Longest Summer*, and *Little Cheung*. *The Runaway Pistol*'s affinity to *Made in Hong Kong* was highlighted in its advertisement. Lam also acquired funding and film stock off-cuts from the mainstream filmmakers such as Andy Lau and Andrew Lau. Stylistically, he is even more experimental than Chan by adopting very mixed modes of representation: a documentary style interwoven with elements of surrealism. Instead of using a totally amateur cast, Lam sought help from his friends in the industry: Barbara Wong, Wilson Yip Wai-shun, and Cheang Pou-soi. He declared this an independent production financed by resources from the mainstream.[33]

Second, the politics of access brings about a cinematic culture of diversity. Alexander Horwath commends Chan as a self-styled Hong Kong indie filmmaker who is very close to the Western idea of the self-conscious contemporary auteur. The most important contribution that Chan has made is to provide a more diversified picture of Hong Kong cinema:

> [I]t is not just brilliantly choreographed action pictures and genre franchise, on the other hand, not just the one-man show of Art God Wong Kar-wai. Rather HK cinema might more and more present itself as a multifaceted terrain that allows for many different aesthetic options which change continuously.[34]

I would add that this practice of independent filmmaking effectuates the democratization of cinematic culture because of the increased diversity of opportunities we have for the contestation of public opinion. Chan's films do not propagandize any socialist ideology of class struggle although the class issue is well foregrounded with constant references to what is often repressed in the grand narrative of the Hong Kong economic miracle.[35] The issues of social and cultural marginality in his films provide an alternative way of historicizing Hong Kong.

These values are closely tied with what Charles Taylor calls "the politics of recognition." Taylor argues that subaltern groups often invoke the notions of equality and dignity so as to achieve their desired recognition.[36] In this kind of subaltern fight, an individual's basic human right to demand a particular mode of authentic self-expression is often emphasized. In her analysis of contemporary Danish cinema in the face of the hegemony of Hollywood globalization, Mette Hjort suggests that authenticity is the "motivating force" behind the influential discourses of subaltern or minority groups.[37] Likewise, in Chan's independent filmmaking, the notion of authenticity is constantly invoked to support the idea of an inwardly generated, authentic self.[38] Yonfan is another exemplary case showing that authenticity is a core value of independent filmmaking. Using his own capital resources, he started his career in the early 1980s as a commercial producer and filmmaker specializing in women's melodramas, featuring glamorous stars like Maggie Cheung, Cherie Chung, and Chow Yun-fat. In the mid-1990s when he turned to risqué subject matters which were "closer to his heart," like transvestites, transsexuality, homosexuality, and sadomasochistic relationships, he began to be regarded as an independent filmmaker.[39]

Social marginality has shaped the construction of imagined communities through the discourse of authenticity. Michael Warner's interesting discussion on counter-publicity may illustrate the point:

> One of the defining elements of modernity . . . is normative stranger-sociability, of a kind that seems to arise only when the social imaginary is defined not by kinship (as in nonstate societies) or by place . . . but by discourse . . . This constitutive and normative environment of strangerhood is more, too, than an objectively describable gesellschaft; it requires our constant imagining.[40]

The constant imagining of being true to oneself helps to circulate the cultural values embraced by those who pursue alternative space within the hegemonic commercial system. This kind of discursive formation binds people across geo-cultural boundaries, shaping what Warner calls "stranger-sociability." The discourses of independence and authenticity become means through which they counter estrangement and isolation. Chan's warm receptions in the overseas film festivals and art-house venues illustrate that films made in Hong Kong have indeed acquired a transnational status, shaping "an imagined community of the indies" throughout the years.[41]

To conclude, it is not easy to draw a clear line between the mainstream and the indie cinema; nor can financial independence guarantee the spirit of autonomy; or to be more precise, there is no absolute independence. However, the corpus of film texts motivated by the urge to achieve authentic self-expression perpetuates the cultural values which foster greater diversity in cinematic culture and inspire more young talents to make films which are not expensive and technology-intensive. Although Chan and others have never produced an independent film movement, it might be interesting to compare them to those from Dogma 95. It is a film movement initiated in 1995 by a group of Danish filmmakers, including Lars von Trier and Thomas Vinterberg, to counter "certain tendencies in the cinema today."[42] While the Dogma filmmakers sought to create an alternative cinematic culture in response to the global encroachment of Hollywood cinema and fostered a strong link between creativity and oppositionality, the "Hong Kong–style" indie filmmakers, who emerged from the 1990s were less organized and politically oppositional, but shared the pursuit of authenticity. The Hong Kong filmmakers, for example, Fruit Chan, Stanley Kwan, Ann Hui, Bryan Chang, Vincent Chui, Carol Lai, and Nelson Yu Lik-wai, have been particularly preoccupied with the possibility of mobilizing "this condition of being true to oneself" to articulate the collective experience of growing up in Hong Kong. Another example of indie filmmaking is Tammy Cheung, who demonstrates strong socio-political consciousness by shooting documentaries on local and political issues with Frederick Wiseman's Direct Cinema style, urging the audience to think about Hong Kong's politics, culture, and society. Transnational elements are found in the works by Evans Chan and

Clara Law, two independent filmmakers with a Hong Kong background. They consistently explore diasporic issues of border-crossing, traveling, migration experiences, identities, and multiculturalism. If the Dogma filmmakers demonstrate a critical response to cinematic globalization, Fruit Chan and the above Hong Kong filmmakers' attempts are more "modest" and less flamboyant, aiming to redefine Hong Kong culture through their creative practices at historically critical moments.

3

There Are Many Ways
to Be Realistic

To try to imitate nature in the representational arts would amount
to wanting to attain an inadequate goal with an inadequate means.

— Victor Shklovsky[1]

Independent and realistic motivations

Although the impossibility of obtaining absolute independence is
our ontological condition, we can identify "independent
motivations" in specific historical times — the moral incentive to
search for independence within constraints. Elsewhere I have
described these historical disjunctures as "moments of danger,"
borrowing from Walter Benjamin, to explore the sense of urgency
that one mobilizes to articulate a disappearing, disjointed time in
history. Such moral incentives interact with creativity to produce
what neo-formalists would call "realistic motivations."[2] This

chapter explores Chan's realist mode in the traditions of Chinese-language cinemas.

To link independent films with realism, however, is sometimes useful and sometimes misleading, depending upon how one defines "realism." Realism as a mode of representation should be studied in specific historical and cultural context. As Kristin Thompson argues, it is not a representational mode which articulates a natural relationship between art and world, nor does it refer to a set of fixed, unchanging traits. Realism as a "formal effect" of the work changes over time as artistic conventions and spectators' viewing skills evolve.[3] Drawing on Russian formalist discussion on defamiliarization, she identifies four types of motivations in artworks, namely compositional, artistic, realistic, and parametric motivations, among which the notion of "realistic motivation" is most relevant in the present discussion. It is a type of textual cue to appeal to our notions of the real world. In Italian neo-realism, for example, some commonly identified "realistic" traits are observed. They include the choice of an amateur cast, the attention to the actual condition of the lower-class people in post-war Italy, and on-location shooting. Nevertheless, as Thompson suggests, "realistic motivation" is more complicated than a set of traits:

> Realistic motivation can never be a natural, unchanging trait of works, however. We always perceive the work against shifting norms. Realism, as a set of formal cues, changes over time, as does any style. It has the ability to be radical and defamiliarizing if the main artistic styles of the time are highly abstract and have become automatized.[4]

Indeed, if realistic motivations appeal to our assumptions about the real world, such ideas are not direct, natural knowledge of the world but are culturally and historically determined. Thompson further points out that realism can be seen as products of defamiliarization in three aspects: everyday reality which is habituated and automatized, grand language which has become the norm, and dominant generic conventions which have dictated spectators' viewing habits. In cases like *Made in Hong Kong*, realism can be perceived as a departure from the norms of popular cinema. Its realist mode has a defamiliarizing capacity which revolts against the dominant gangster genre popularized by the *Young and Dangerous* series in the mid-1990s. Chan himself has the following to say about the series and his motivation to challenge the dominant film mode:

> [W]hen I analyzed the series from a moral perspective, I found the messages they preached were in fact contaminating. Since the series was a huge box-office hit, I thought people would grow to become this way, and so would our society. I once heard a mother calling a radio phone-in program, praising it as a good film. If parents also lacked the ability to decipher the ideology behind this film, our society was at a moment of danger. If I shot a film just like the *Young and Dangerous* series, about a "triad-kid" hero who pretended to be smart and courageous, it would be no different from them. So I decided to destabilize that heroic point-of-view. Moon ostensibly seemed to be a hero, but in the end he was just a loser. His monologues at the very end of the film were in fact self-reflections, criticizing himself. If I hadn't come across that mother's phone call on the radio, I might have taken up the traditional heroism central to Hong Kong cinema, and probably wouldn't have dealt with the issue in such depth.[5]

We can reiterate that realism is less concerned with a set of identifiable traits than a means for filmmakers to actualize their independent motivations. Realism in film does not necessarily guarantee a critical and oppositional stance. For some critics, the emergence of the *Young and Dangerous* series signifies a more realistic turn from the previous heroic gangster genre, often called *yingxiongpian.* Li Cheuk-to claims that on-location shooting and sound synchronization in the young gangster films enhanced the sense of realism, and its shift to youth power addresses what is missed in reality.[6] However, the youthful heroic mode employed in these films, very much a recycled element from its *yingxiongpian* predecessors, seems to confirm the ideology rather than challenge it. However, in *Made in Hong Kong*, realistic motivations are associated with opposition and subversion. Meaning is not divorced from form; realism is utilized not solely to express meaning but to create defamiliarization which helps to mediate one's own agency in a world dominated by commercial constraints. The next chapter explores the way realism has been mobilized as a device to challenge and defamiliarize the popular gangster genre.

All art forms are products of defamiliarization and even *cinema vérité* requires selection and interpretation, but reality and realism should be clearly distinguished. There are in fact many modes of realism and Chan's case illustrates this concept clearly. His so-called "Handover Trilogy" and his later films such as *Durian Durian* and *Hollywood Hong Kong* embody certain basic traits: the story of ordinary people, the theme of marginality, on-location shooting, jerky hand-held camerawork, frequent use of objective point of view camera, and the casting of non-professional actors. All these characteristics have led critics to conclude that he belongs safely to the tradition of social realism and that Hong Kong through his lens is a "real" one.[7] While Chan's realism excites critics because of its opposition to mainstream cinematic conventions, the mixed use of documentary realism and illusionism confuses the same cohort. Bono Lee was one of the first critics to argue that Chan is not realistic; in his view, Chan's aesthetics are better described as "dramatic realism" because of exaggerated plot elements. Other critics also notice his constant use of surrealistic images.[8] In an interview, Chan argued that his film style is more aptly described as "quasi-realistic":

This issue about realism is what I always argue with critics about. I think I'm not solely a realist as it's implausible to reach the kind of realism that can be seen in Iranian films, or mainland Chinese films . . . My films could be termed as "quasi-realism" or "half realism and half fabricated realism," which could mean that they're "fake realism." But with my films, take *Made in Hong Kong* as an example, how can they be categorized? To be frank, they can't because up to sixty percent of the plot is based on real-life events. The innovative part lies in the use of non-professional actors, which is also a technique employed by neo-realists . . . So those veteran film critics get themselves into trouble. They have preconceived notions of what realism and neo-realism is, but using these models of the 1960s to weigh or compare my films makes for inevitable discrepancies.[9]

The mixed mode of representation in his films includes realistic traits which create and enhance the impressions and effects of the real, as well as illusionistic and even surrealistic elements. In Chapter 6 when we discuss this mixed mode of realism, we will show that the dramatic and surrealistic elements are significant "artistic and compositional motivations," to borrow Thompson's terminology, which help to undermine one's sense of certainty about reality at a moment of critical transition. They help to cue the audience to realize the conundrum of the "real" at a mutating moment. "Quasi-realism" enables filmmakers to acknowledge their own limitations to articulate their self-identities during a process of mutation, and provides them with greater freedom to project their imagination about their future.

Chan's notion of "quasi-realism" shares some attributes of the realist movement which has emerged in contemporary Chinese-language cinemas. As aesthetic responses to unprecedented changes in the history of Chinese people in the postsocialist era, realist films from the so-called "Urban Generation" also embody realistic motivations. However, as Jia Zhangke argues, such drastic changes cannot be easily captured by a documentary mode of representation. In an interview, when he was asked whether the 1980s could be regarded as a time of void when there were no records of visual memory of his generation, Jia claimed that it was due to a sense of loss and melancholy that he made films like *The Pickpocket* (1997) and *Platform* (2000) as a kind of compensation to fill up that void:

> What I mean by "documentary" is not only the "record" of reality but also the "remembering" of people's feelings and thoughts, even the most fantastical ones . . . I made these films because I wanted to compensate for what was not fulfilled. I must also emphasize that apart from the realist mode, there are other kinds of representation that can be called "visual memory," for example, Dali's surrealist images in the early twentieth century can be grouped under psychological realism.[10]

While Jia himself admits that his films are "realistic," there exist many different modes of realism which aim to capture the "real." In critical reaction to the Fifth Generation filmmakers who use film for mere depiction of legends, Jia believes in realism as an effective strategy which generates "the effects of the real," rather than the faithful reflection of the unattainable "real."[11] He once explained why the feature *Still Life* (2006) was made after the documentary film *Dong* (2006), both of which are about the Three Gorges Dam: "it is not a bad thing to learn about the limitations of documentary."[12] Jia did not say so explicitly but one can infer why a mixed mode of representation seems to be preferred by filmmakers caught up in times of great changes.

The combination of "realistic and independent motivations" makes film art less a "faithful" record of reality than a hermeneutical endeavor to make sense of the changing world and to resolve what cannot be fulfilled in real life.[13] This is especially true with film practitioners who work outside or at the edge of the dominant mainstream discourse. Realistic films, whether "independent" or not, are alternative, if not oppositional, practices. This emphasis on agency confirms that artistic and cultural representations are not merely an effect of language. As artists and moral subjects, filmmakers cannot evade linguistic mediation but they can speak about their moral intuitions and existentialist incentives to make sense of the world.[14]

Fruit Chan and cinematic realism in Chinese-language cinemas

To better understand realism in Chan's films, it's beneficial to take a "long shot" and a "close-up" of his mode in the tradition of cinematic realism in Chinese-language cinemas. The "long shot" explores how his position in the tradition deviates from socialist-realist and realistic-nationalistic discourses. The "close-up" links his work to practices of social realism in Hong Kong cinema since the 1970s.

Discussing various forms of realism in Chinese cinema, Chris Berry and Mary Farquhar observe:

> Realism was originally hailed as a radical aesthetic that was grounded in secular cosmologies whose core is social transformation. Transformation as *telos* is the crux of scientific and supposedly universal meta-narratives that dominated twentieth-century Chinese thought and cinema: Social Darwinism and then Marxism-Leninism.[15]

This early connection often leads critics to associate films of social realism depicting subject matter of social concern with socialist realism, although the two should be differentiated from each other. Social realism in film refers to representations engaging subjects of social concern while socialist realism is a teleologically-oriented style of realistic art which seeks to pursue specific goals of socialism and communism. In this light, Chan's films embody some traits of social, if not socialist, realism in the history of Chinese cinemas. His concern for underprivileged people and social injustice brings him close to this realist tradition. Chan's films are not always characterized by an insider's sympathy but rather a critical distance which portrays the powerlessness and weaknesses of the marginalized. Some of his characters, for example in *Durian Durian* and *Little Cheung*, have the flair of ordinariness, very similar to those in Jia's films, while others are quite exotic and symbolic, for example the obese family in *Hollywood Hong Kong* and the characters in *Dumplings*. Even in his debut *Made in Hong Kong*, in which all actors are non-professional, the characters' lives are tragically dramatic, sharing the sensationalism of Hong Kong actor-director Patrick Lung Kong's films of social relevance in the 1970s. Issues such as crime, prostitution, and drug abuse are central to Lung's representative films. Stephen Teo observes that Lung's films integrate "the didacticism of the 60s and the more exploitative 70s realism."[16] Lung's films like *Story of a Discharged Prisoner* (1967), *Teddy Girls* (1969), and *The Call Girls* (1973) appeared at a time when Chinese cinema was dominated by the kung fu and martial arts genres. Teo further argues that this kind of timing shows that Lung was unwilling to compromise with the dominant trend of filmmaking.[17] One may say similar things about Chan. His use of sometimes exaggerated and farcical scenes reminds viewers of his familiarity with Hong Kong commercial film modes. However, his persistent attempts to articulate social and cultural mutations through the experience of the marginalized subvert the heroic mode popularized by the dominant action and gangster genres.

In comparative light, some notable films about disaffected youth in the international cinema can be cited. Chan once acknowledged that Japanese filmmaker Nagisa Oshima is his influence.[18] The bleak destiny of the youth in Oshima's *Cruel Tragedy of Youth* echoes with those in *Made in Hong Kong*. If Oshima's disillusionment with the political left is noticeable in his portrayal of the destructive youth, Chan constantly casts doubts on the capacity of the lower-class people to engage in a utopian socialist struggle. Oshima was also fond of mixing farce and satire together, for example in *Death by Hanging* (1968). Other comparisons emerge with Luis Buñuel's *The Forgotten Ones* (*Los Olvidados*) which portrays the life of some juvenile delinquents in the slums of Mexico City. The protagonist Pedro is abandoned by his parents and has to steal food from home. In a helpless state, he faces an environment of poverty, violence, cruelty, and crime. Despair prolongs even after the end of the film as his body is dumped as rubbish in a ditch. Mathieu Kassovitz's *Hate* (*La Haine*, 1995) follows three teenage friends (a Jew, an African, and an Arab) hanging around on the Paris outskirts in a span of twenty-four hours. In the aftermath of a riot, their conflicts with the policemen lead to the tragic death of one of them. Another tale about alienated youth, Sofia Coppola's *The Virgin Suicides* (1999) narrates the mass suicide of five sisters in an affluent suburb of Detroit in the 1970s. It addresses the unhappiness, solitude, and fragile lives of adolescent girls although the characters in Coppola's film do not fall into the lower stratum of society.

The social realism in *Made in Hong Kong* also finds echoes in some examples of the cinemas of Taiwan and the PRC during times of critical transition in Chinese communities. Edward Yang's *A Brighter Summer Day* (1991) is mainly about the killing of a young school girl by a school boy in Taipei in the early 1960s. It depicts the life of teenage gangs and their search for identity at a time when Taiwan's political future was unclear. Filmed in postsocialist China, Jia's *Unknown Pleasures* (2002) illustrates the mundane lives of two unemployed young men in Datong, "City of Coal," in northern China. They wander the city and eventually commit robbery. Going nowhere, they envisage no optimistic future for themselves in the wake of relentless modernization and globalization in contemporary China.

These films of disaffected youth share a clear deviation from socialist idealism which has a certain propagandistic bent and utopian vision. Apart from this, Chan does not express strong interest in the valorization of the realist-nationalist discourse. In recent scholarship on Chinese cinemas, the common view holds that cinematic realism is a major strand of nationalist discourses and Cold War ideology, whether referring to socialist realism in mainland China in the 1950s and 60s or "Healthy Realism" in Taiwan around the same time.[19] In such cases, when the individual is posited in the background of modernity and nationhood, the pursuit of a "realist-nationalist" style is also ideologically imbued. In comparative light, Chan's films articulate a discourse differentiated from this strand of realism. *Made in Hong Kong* can be considered as a social drama about youth crime and a story of growing up. Both types of film embody strong "realistic motivations" to deal with issues of urban Hong Kong. Youth crime had become a prominent theme by the early 1980s, and many Hong Kong New Wave films have strong political undertones. Tsui Hark's *Dangerous Encounter — First Kind* (1980), Yim Ho's *The Happenings* (1980), Alex Cheung's *Man on the Brink* (1981), and Patrick Tam's *Nomad* (1982) have been regarded as the most representative films of this genre. At about the same time, youth crime was a favorite subject for the Radio Television Hong Kong (RTHK) television drama series. Examples include Rachel Zen's *See You on the Other Side* (1981) — which some argue was the prototype for David Lai's *Lonely Fifteen* (1982) — and Andrew Lau's *Young and Dangerous* series in the 1990s. Lawrence Lau's *Gangs* (1988), made in a docu-drama mode, has been regarded as a classic example of realistic portrayal of young people growing up in a triad society. His more recent production *Spacked Out* (2000) uses a docu-drama approach to capture the life-style of four teen girls in a satellite city in Hong Kong. Their everyday activities revolve around karaoke, shopping, fighting, drugs, sex, and abortion. It presents a hopeless state of youth culture. These films provide a platform for social criticism of the government's negligence of marginalized youth. Ng Ho is right to point out that youth crime as a theme in New Wave Cinema in the early 1980s is not accidental; it reveals the collective consciousness of New Wave directors, locally born and bred, exploring the cultural specificities of Hong Kong. In these films, youth are depicted as marginalized people who are uneducated, unemployed, or abandoned by families. These films show, Ng suggests, that in a violent society, young people use violence as a means of survival.[20] The youth crime genre of course is a sub-genre of stories of growing up in which the protagonists do not necessarily commit crime but run into conflict with social values borne by older generations. Allen Fong's *Father and Son* (1981) and *Ah Ying* (1983) are exemplary, as well as television programs produced by the film workers from RTHK.

One can argue that social realism in Hong Kong cinema is an effective style of delivering an urban historiography. *Made in Hong Kong*, like its predecessors in the cinemas of Hong Kong and elsewhere, narrates the frustrating experience of growing up in colonial Hong Kong. The sense of homelessness expressed paradoxically conveys a sense of place. Although the urban space in this shared filmic world of urban imaginary is characterized by an aestheticization of violence, the Hong Kong city is also the "quotidian space" of growing up, in Henri Lefebvre's sense of the world. It is a place one calls "home," despite how precarious and homeless one may feel. This sense of place is clearly distinguishable from the transient identity represented in films and literary works of the 1950s and 60s, which critics have called "the southbound imaginary" to refer to cultural representations of southbound migrants from mainland China during wartime and especially during and after the Communist takeover in 1949.[21] Many of the southbound writers or filmmakers perceive Hong Kong as a stopover while imagining China as a distant imaginary homeland. Contrary to this vision, urban realism constructs a sense of place by way of yearning for a home which is constantly subject to mutation, exploitation, and uprootedness. I call this urban vision "the ghostly city" and explore its specificities in Chapters 5 and 6.

Urban realism in Hong Kong films is therefore not the same as the urban cinema in Shanghai in the 1920s and 30s. In tracing the "Urban Generation" in contemporary mainland China to the tradition of "a city-oriented cinema" in Shanghai in the beginning of the twentieth century, Zhang Zhen remarks that Shanghai urban modernity was not only the background of the films of the 1920s and 30s but also the key element in form and content of those films:

> While the process of intensified modernization resulted in the flourishing of a metropolitan material civilization, it also brought about a great gap between the rich and the poor, class differences, the intensification of gender politics, and the struggle and resistance of local culture against the onslaught of Western culture.[22]

In this regard, Zhang suggests that the emergence of contemporary urban filmmakers in the PRC echoes with the early Shanghai tradition. These film traditions express the paradoxical nature of modernity that Marshall Berman earlier called "life's possibilities and perils."[23] While this general observation also pertains to Hong Kong's urban cinema, Chan's films do not articulate explicit anti-Western, nationalistic sentiments as counter-discourses to the waves of postmodernizations. There may be subtle critiques of the then-colonial British government but the self-reflective stance toward such "onslaught" exposes the weaknesses and helpless condition of the underprivileged. Many of his characters are those who are caught up with the waves of globalization, consuming commodities and "benefiting" from global capitalism while at the same time suffering from its uneven developments. Even the artisan characters, like Yan (Qin Hailu) in *Durian Durian*, are not always upbeat and never heroic. Gradually and systematically the "national" is displaced in the film discourse of the urban where nostalgic urban dwellers lament the passing of time in the ruins of the city.

In this chapter, the notion of "motivation" is understood in relation to the film-practitioners' moral intent and the film's formal properties. It is through these two levels of meaning that we can understand how auteurism and creativity can combine to produce films of critical nature. *Made in Hong Kong* is one outstanding example of this endeavor.

4

The Art of *Détournement*

When a newly independent art paints its world in brilliant colors,
then a moment of life has grown old. By art's brilliant colors it
cannot be rejuvenated but only recalled to mind. The greatness
of art makes its appearance only as dusk begins to fall over life.

— Guy Debord[1]

Class consciousness and the art of *détournement*

Culture is an ongoing process of renewal and negation. In his
discussion of hegemony and structures of feeling, Raymond
Williams outlines a relation between the dominant and the residual,
and between the dominant and the emergent. In both cases, the
relation of emergent and residual cultural formations to the
dominant can roughly be understood as alternative and
oppositional. While the dominant is always hegemonic enough to

incorporate or repress the other two in political or commercial contexts, the emergent and the residual may coexist with the dominant in the same cultural space in an ongoing process of renewal and negation. Independent filmmaking is illustrative of this process as the emergent is often referred to as what is innovative and new that "pops" up at a moment of time. In some cases, emergent cultural formations can also be bound up with oppositional and avant-garde stances of art cinema. The previous chapter noted how realism can be tied with emergent, innovative, and radical forces. The defamiliarizing power of realist films makes them oppositional and critical. In a similar way, with its "realistic motivations," *Made in Hong Kong* embodies the defamiliarizing effect, setting off a series of efforts of artistic *détournement*.[2]

The French Situationists talked about the art of *détournement* as a response to the problems brought about by mass culture, or what Guy Debord aptly coins as "the society of the spectacle." Debord describes it as a "dialectical movement," which is manifested by the "*reversal* of established relationships between concepts and by the diversion (or *détournement*) of all the attainments of earlier critical efforts."[3] He further states:

> *Détournement* is the antithesis of quotation of a theoretical authority invariably tainted if only because it has become quotable, because it is now a fragment torn away from its context, from its own movement, and ultimately from the overall frame of reference of its period and from the precise option that it constituted within that framework. *Détournement*, by contrast, is the fluid language of anti-ideology. It occurs within a type of communication aware of its inability to enshrine any inherent and definitive certainty. This language is inaccessible in the highest degree to confirmation by any earlier or supra-critical reference point. On the contrary, its internal coherence and its adequacy in respect of the practically possible are what validate the ancient kernel of truth that it restores. *Détournement* founds

its cause on nothing but its own truth as critique at work in the present.[4]

To put it simply, *détournement* can be understood as the "recycling, re-positioning, or re-employing of the existing elements of an art work, or works, into a new synthesis."[5] This kind of diversion must grant the new text its autonomy and original significance. In some cases, the project of *détournement* entails a communist-socialist orientation in which the consciousness of class can be discerned. In her discussion of Hong Kong cinema's transnationality, Meaghan Morris cites a French Situationist film called *Can Dialectics Break Bricks?* made by René Viénet in 1973. Viénet and his colleagues recycled a Hong Kong martial arts film by removing its soundtrack and "hilariously substituted for it an anarcho-Marxist reading in French of the entire image-track as though the film were an allegory of class struggle between 'proletarians' and 'bureaucrats'."[6]

As mentioned before, the class consciousness inherent in *Made in Hong Kong* does not directly pertain to any Marxist allegory of class struggle. Without a utopian vision in the socialist-realist tradition, the film focuses on the "cruel tragedy of the youth" in the changing space of Hong Kong. Despite this difference, *Made in Hong Kong* relates to the idea of *détournement* because of Fruit Chan's incentives to articulate an alternative and critical vision within Hong Kong's commercial cinema. "Realistic motivations" in the film are main devices which make *détournement* possible but what Kristin Thompson calls "transtextual motivations" cannot be ignored. Transtextual motivation "involves any appeal to conventions of other artworks, and hence it can be as varied as the historical circumstances allow."[7] In films, the most common transtextual devices depend on our knowledge of the same genre, of the star, or of similar conventions in other artworks. Other critics have referred to this as intertextuality — "a special type which preexists the artwork, and upon which the artist may draw in a straightforward or playful way."[8] The process of *détournement* relies on the ways that realistic motivations are used intertextually to challenge our assumptions by subverting genre conventions.

The spectacle of the *Young and Dangerous* series and its speedy responses

It is well known that *Made in Hong Kong* was a critical response to the *Young and Dangerous* series, the dominant Hong Kong commercial gangster film series in the mid-1990s. The first *Young and Dangerous* was very popular, with five sequels and one prequel within a short span of five years.[9] Its legendary characters and plotlines were based on a comic strip series *Teddy Boy*, which came out in 1992 and has been very popular among the local youngsters. It revolves around Chan Ho-nam, Chicken, and Ho-nam's other comrades in the Hung Hing triad gang. They are childhood friends who grew up together in Tsz Wan Shan, one of the oldest and biggest public housing estates in Hong Kong. Ho-nam's adherence to traditional values such as brotherhood and righteousness makes him a rising star in the gang. The comic strip appeals to youngsters because of his youthful image and character traits.

Andrew Lau, the director of the *Young and Dangerous* series, started his career as an assistant cinematographer for the Shaw Brothers studio in the early 1980s. He has been renowned for shooting action scenes using hand-held camerawork. He was the cinematographer for Wong Kar-wai's *As Tears Go By* (1988) and worked with Christopher Doyle as co-cinematographer in *Chungking Express* (1994) and *Fallen Angels* (1995). One may discern that the prototype of Ho-nam was the young triad hero Wah (Andy Lau) in *As Tears Go By*. Lau began to direct films in 1991 and his first box-office hit was *Young and Dangerous*. He made many box-office successes at a time when Hong Kong's film industry was in a downturn.[10] His most acclaimed film is *Infernal Affairs* (2002), which Martin Scorsese remade as *The Departed* (2006).

The box-office success of the *Young and Dangerous* series was attributed to Lau's sensitivity to the needs of the local film market. He introduced some innovative elements to gangster films, which were appealing to viewers in Hong Kong. Since the series was based on *Teddy Boy*, many local youngsters were drawn to the films because of their identification with the comic righteous heroes. The films celebrate the spirit of teamwork, rather than individual heroism. Very often, it is through the co-operation of the young gang members that law and order in the triad society is sustained. Lau cast upcoming young idols to play the main characters, including Ekin Cheng as Ho-nam and Jordan Chan as Chicken. Their trendy and stylish outfits were a major attraction to young audiences. The series was made with a low budget, but with professional shooting skills. The plot is not complex, the story is delivered at a fast pace, and the fighting scenes are often spectacular. In addition, the romantic plotline and numerous funny gimmicks further popularized the series.

The first three parts of the series, which were shown in 1996, set down the basic traits of the plot — righteousness and betrayal. *Young and Dangerous 1* opens with the younger days of Ho-nam, Chicken, and their childhood friends in the public housing estate. They were bullied by "Ugly Kwan" (Francis Ng), but saved by Bee (Ng Chi-hung) who later became their "Big Brother" in the Hung Hing gang. Young Ho-nam's righteousness and calmness are well praised by the gang's leaders. When Ho-nam is competing against "Ugly Kwan" as "the branch leader" in Causeway Bay, he is framed by the latter for murdering Bee. Ho-nam's loyalty to the gang is then well tested, and at the same time Chicken is forced to flee to Taiwan. Later, with the help of Chicken and his gang members from Taiwan, Ho-nam kills "Ugly Kwan" in revenge for Bee. He is then appointed as the branch leader in Causeway Bay.

In *Young and Dangerous 2*, Ho-nam has conflicts with Tai Fei (Anthony Wong) in the same gang since he has taken charge of Causeway Bay. With the use of flashback, the story tells how Chicken becomes a branch leader in San Luen, the largest gang in Taiwan. The gang's boss, Liu (Lei Zhen), attempts to expand his gambling business in Macao, creating tension between San Luen and Hung Hing. Chicken has an affair with Ting Yiu (Chingmy Yau), the mistress of Liu, but he is framed by her for murdering Liu. With the help of Ho-nam and Tai Fei, Ting Yiu's betrayal is uncovered and she is shot to death by Chicken. Hung Hing maintains its power in Macao.

Young and Dangerous 3 begins with the Tung Sing gang's attempt to expand its power to Hung Hing's territories. The expansion is driven by a fierce young man, Crow (Roy Cheung). In Crow's rise to power, he murders Ho-nam's girlfriend and the two bosses of Hung Hing and Tung Sing. Ho-nam is framed for the murders of the bosses, but he is well trusted by his comrades. In the funeral of Tung Sing's boss, Crow's conspiracy is uncovered and he is killed in a spectacular fight among the triad gangs.

The celebration of youth power is most remarkable, resulting in the further popularization of the "Teddy Boy" image in the popular comic strip series in Hong Kong. Not only was the image of Ho-nam an instant hit overnight, the stylish images of the other young gangsters also attracted popular attention. As minor and supporting characters for the older gangsters in heroic films, as in John Woo's films, these young gangsters are amplified, assuming major roles in the series.

In response to the popularity of the *Young and Dangerous* series, some interesting texts emerged in Hong Kong visual culture, aiming to divert, twist, and turn away from the "spectacle" constructed by the series. In the commercial circuit, Cha Chuen-yee's *Once Upon a Time in Triad Society 1* and *2* (both 1996) and Wilson Yip Wai-shun's *Mongkok Story* (1996) parody the myth of the young gangsters. In the more alternative space, we can find Chan's *Made in Hong Kong*, Doreen Etzler's video *Film 2 HK 1995* (1999), and Lam Wah-chuen's *The Runaway Pistol*. Etzler's work is one of the interesting shorts in the Videotage project called *Star City — The Best of Videotage Volume 6*. With its focus on Hong Kong urban space, *Star City* showcased a selection of examples of "artists' negotiation of the space which surrounds us, from hyper-architecture to spatio-temporal dislocations to the cinematic spectacle and back."[11] Lam Wah-chuen's film with financial support from Andy Lau, on the other hand, is closer to Chan's *Made in Hong Kong* in its mode of filmmaking. Although the techniques of *détournement* differ enormously among these films, they all manifest a common concern to re-employ commercial elements to redefine the culture of Hong Kong; among them, Chan's film is the most influential endeavor in the space between the alternative and the mainstream.

In considering the speedy interactions mentioned above, Lisa Odham Stokes and Michael Hoover observe that the young triad gang formula in Hong Kong cinema in the 1990s appeared at a time when the industry began to decline, generating short-term big revenues. They have noted that a global network of flexible accumulation characterized the modes of production as there were new efforts to manipulate market demand, such as film premiers, appearances of actors in concerts, and tie-in soundtracks. In addition, the speed with which these films and their parodic versions were produced "indicates an acceleration in the development of film-as-commodity, epitomizing late capital and its cultural logic."[12] While it is true that the notion of flexible accumulation shows how global capitalism worked in Hong Kong cinema in the 1990s, the rapid reproduction and imitation of sequels have been a notorious feature of Hong Kong film industry ever since the 1960s. Generic formulas have always been exploited extensively in the industry. But this kind of "metacultural acceleration" can also be located at the edge of the mainstream.[13] Various efforts of *détournement*, caught up in this whirlwind of speedy reproduction, open up alternative visions of articulating heroism. Speedy reproductions did not save the waning Hong Kong film industry from its downturn; nevertheless, they stimulated critical reactions at an important stage of Hong Kong's independent filmmaking and helped expand the cinematic public sphere both locally and transnationally.[14]

Recoding heroism in the *jianghu*

Made in Hong Kong expresses a clear intention to recode the meaning of *jianghu* in the context of gangster films. The strategies of repositioning the generic elements in the *Young and Dangerous* series demonstrate a radical shift from the portrayal of a comic version of the *jianghu* to a tragic one. The notion of *jianghu* originates from martial arts fiction, literally means "rivers and lakes" in Chinese, and normally refers to the "self-contained and historically sanctioned world of martial arts."[15] In Chinese-language films, *jianghu* therefore is understood as "an imaginary world of signification that operates under the sign of swordplay films."[16] The notion of heroism is basic to the formation of this cultural construct since traditionally swordsmen who traverse this space are supposed to be morally intact heroes. The idea of *jianxia*, which is "swordsman" in Chinese, indicates someone who is heroic and admirable. In connection with this, virtues such as loyalty and fraternity are attributes of these martial arts heroes. Without doubt, martial arts films are comparable to Western morality plays where the code of good and bad is sustained.[17] Drawing on the foundational texts on the study of martial arts fiction and films,

Stephen Ching-kiu Chan remarks, "As a discursive world *jianghu* has come to symbolize the race for excellence and power; it provides in turn the symbolic context necessary for the material circulation of an imaginary of human desires conducive to the search for excellence and power."[18]

In Hong Kong film history, this discursive world has found its fullest manifestation in the *wuxia* genre, which contains basically sword fighting in a medieval imaginary world. Classic examples include King Hu and Chang Cheh's films produced in the 1960s and 70s. Tsui Hark and Ching Siu-tung are two other *wuxia* masters who have made many films in this genre since the late 1970s.[19] The extension of this notion of *jianghu* from the medieval swordplay to the urban gangster genre shows how the *wuxia* films have been reinvented and modernized. The *Young and Dangerous* series clearly follows the formula popularized by Woo's "heroic" gangster films in its interpretation of *jianghu*. The major difference is the celebration of youth power in the young gangster film. The underworld of the triad society in both types of film does not merely embody the characteristics of the medieval *jianghu*; it is a modernized version of it.

Apart from this urge to excel and compete for power, the triad society is represented as a *jianghu* in a modern and urban setting. In gangster films, it is a self-contained imaginary world of signification as it is completely separated from the so-called "normal," lawful society. As a kind of miniaturized society with its own law, order, and hierarchy, it takes on some traditional Chinese values which are in no way residual. Values such as loyalty and fraternity have assumed a central position in the cosmic order of triad society. They are also mobilized to sustain the hierarchical and patriarchal structure within the triad gang. The practice of worshipping the legendary figure Kwan Yu (the Chinese god of war) in *Young and Dangerous 1*, for example, reinforces the virtue of loyalty; consequently any challenge to the leader is not permissible.

The film does include Ugly Kwan, who seeks to challenge the Big Brother's authority by proposing the possibility of an election of the leader. However, since this character is represented as a villain, there is no attempt to uphold modern liberal values such as democracy.[20] There is a strong urge to search for a lost father (authority) and the ultimate aim is to restore the cosmic order that has been disrupted by various negative forces, including betrayal, jealousy, greed, and cruelty. At the end of the film, after the villain is killed, the original leader is reinstated although there has been some mention that the young gangster leader Ho-nam should take charge. The film closes with the restoration of the status quo in the underworld. This ending is a comic one because the conflictual forces are ultimately resolved and a state of equilibrium is reasserted. The protagonist's symbolic homecoming is also clearly implied.

The young heroes, as Li Cheuk-to points out, "had learned the lessons of the older generation and could take over the running of the organization, elevating its status in society and securing law and order."[21] Their heroic images are not less impressive than the older gangsters in Woo's "classics." Ekin Cheng, playing the role of the young gangster leader Ho-nam, is a cool and stylish model to the young people who are also familiar with the comic strip *Teddy Boy* discussed earlier (figs. 4.1a–4.1c). His black leather outfit and hairstyle were chic at the time of its release. The young gangsters' claim of power is demonstrated in the film's theme song emphasizing their ability to take charge of the (under)world. The song, written in Chinese, can be translated as "I can take charge." A few lines from the song lyrics will illustrate this kind of heroic celebration of youthful rigor and vigor: "I am making huge achievements / I claim that I can take charge . . . / The youth are in charge of this area / The youth are the best."[22]

Figure 4.1a *Young and Dangerous 1*: Ekin Cheng as Chan Ho-nam.

Figure 4.1b The character of Chan Ho-nam is introduced to the audience with a freeze frame . . .

Figure 4.1c . . . and a comic image.

As Debord argues, *détournement* is a process of recontextualization; the original text has become quotable because the new text is an antithesis to it. The most antithetical movement in *Made in Hong Kong* is the diversion from the heroic order and the patriarchal structure sustained in the gangster's *jianghu*. The significance of the film is found in its ability to critically dialogue with the Hong Kong cinematic productions from which it quotes, recycles, and repositions.

In the *Young and Dangerous* series, when the young people are no different from the typical martial arts heroes who compete for excellence in the *jianghu*, the triad society has become only a trope or a figure of speech rather than an actual social context. The ritualistic function of heroism is thus enacted in this tropic world of the *jianghu*. As heroism and fantasy are closely related, heroism helps to sustain an illusion of reality and maintain what in the literary context is called "the suspension of disbelief." To more fully understand how heroism in fiction and film functions, we can turn to what is commonly understood as the game dimension of formulas. John Cawelti suggests that the "object of the game is to get the hero to lend his force to the good group and to destroy the villain." He thinks that there are two aspects in this game dimension:

> First, there is the patterned experience of excitement, suspense, and release which we associate with the functions of entertainment and recreation. Second, there is the aspect of play as ego-enhancement through the temporary resolution of inescapable frustrations and tensions through fantasy.[23]

Realism as defamiliarization

Made in Hong Kong shows a departure from this heroic and romantic ideal, weakening the ritualistic function that Cawelti talks about. All the youngsters in the film can be regarded as failures in life, and in fact they all end in death in one way or another. Moon, Sylvester, Ping, and Susan, who are abandoned by adults, are useful devices for Chan to reposition the problem youths in the actual social and cultural context where they arise. It is clearly due to the use of "realistic motivations" that this kind of recontextualization is possible. In the first instance, the self-contained triad society is now decentered, losing its metaphoric function. It is the actual social context of the youngsters which matters more in the film. In fact, except Moon who can be remotely considered as a member of the gang, Ping and Sylvester play the roles of victims in the triad society. The former's family is harassed by the triad gang because of her father's inability to pay debts while the latter, mentally-handicapped, has little use but to serve as a scapegoat in the gang. Susan, the girl who committed suicide, has absolutely no relationship with the gang. Instead of following the classic Hollywood narrative in which the dramatic action springs primarily from individual characters as causal agents, the youngsters in *Made in Hong Kong* are better seen as victims of Hong Kong society. There is less emphasis on their decisions and choices than on what they cannot do. They lack the desire to achieve, a basic character trait that gets the classic mode of narrative moving. In heroic tales, the characters' action is motivated by a desire to achieve a goal.[24] On the contrary, the poor youngsters in this film are trapped in an unchanging state of homelessness in a changing city. The ways in which the domestic and urban spaces are depicted as hauntingly repetitive is discussed in the next chapter. Moon's involvement in the triad society does not provide him a chance to assume the role of the hero in a game that Cawelti suggested before. When their desires are portrayed, they are represented as highly eroticized and linked only to the youthful yearning for relationship-building, which, in the final instance, ends in tragic death.

Amateurism in casting, ironically necessitated by Chan's lack of resources, is another important trait which weakens the ritualistic function of heroes in the triad society/*jianghu*. Sam Lee, who played

Moon, was literally a boy in the street. Ping and Susan are also amateur actresses while Sylvester was played by one of the crew members. The use of non-professional actors and actresses, like on-location shooting, renders a more down-to-earth and "realistic" *mise-en-scène*. The realistic cues, resulting from "independent motivations," ironically enhance the film's critical capacity. As protagonist of the film, Moon is the most prominent example of anti-heroism. Lacking Ekin Cheng's star quality, Lee looks ordinary, unattractive, and mundane, compared to other Hong Kong action heroes such as Chow Yun-fat and Jackie Chan (fig. 4.2). The latter was used as Moon's pretext for not working hard and misbehaving. After Moon's mother discovers that Moon has stolen her money, she makes the following comment:

> Every time I told him to go to school, he would use Jackie Chan as an example to contradict me. I don't care how he [Jackie Chan] got his master's degree without ever studying in a university. Do you realize what he does? He's an actor, stupid?[25]

The action hero fails to serve as a successful role model; its myth is finally deconstructed.

Figure 4.2   *Made in Hong Kong*: Sam Lee as Moon.

Moon's anti-heroism is also manifested in his use of a pistol. The use of a weapon can be a tool of empowerment for the weak in *jianghu*, but a weapon in his hand becomes a tool of disempowerment. To raise money for Ping to cure her kidney illness, Moon promises to kill two businessmen from Shenzhen. For the "triad boys" in the *Young and Dangerous* series, killing a person signifies their entry into adulthood. The job could be a coming-of-age ritual for Moon too, if he completes it properly. Moon indulges himself in playing with the pistol at home, in a state of self-hypnosis where he loses himself in fantasy with background psychedelic music suggesting a sense of unreality. In this scene, there are several shots set in extremely light, blank background, focusing attention on the stylish ways that Moon holds the pistol. His body image is almost entirely in silhouette. Spotlights on the movie posters on the wall reveal close-ups of Oliver Stone's *Natural Born Killers* (1994) and Luc Besson's *Leon the Professional* (1994). *Natural Born Killers* tells how a serial killer couple, Mickey and Mallory, is glamorized by the media and become heroes. The killer in *Leon the Professional* is also depicted as a hero. He saves a young girl from danger and later loses his life in a fatal battle against the enemies of her family. Moon imitates Mickey and Leon by wearing sunglasses, both at home and then at the tram station while carrying out the mission. Together with Jackie Chan, these heroic images demonstrate how youngsters' self-perceptions are shaped by local and international media.

Despite his efforts to imitate, when Moon meets the two businessmen face to face in the tram station on the Peak, he is in a great panic and fails the trial. Chan depicts Moon's actions in two intriguing sequences. In the first, he looks brave and upbeat all the way. The shots of Moon running towards the businessmen and then running away are in slow-motion movement (fig. 4.3a). They remind viewers of Woo's aestheticization of violence and heroism in *The Killer* (1989). Inserted between these actions is a shot of a tram running downhill, with an off-screen sound like a pistol firing.

In the second sequence with similar actions, Moon looks nervous. Fast-paced movements suggest that he is at a loss; the non-diegetic music at a faster beat creates an ambience of danger and risk. This second sequence reveals that he has not fired the pistol. In a long shot, Moon runs downhill along the tramway in a fright (fig. 4.3b). The viewers then come to know that the first sequence could be Moon's fantasy. Toward the end of the film, to avenge Sylvester and himself, Moon decides to perish together with the enemies. He is "heroic" enough to use the pistol to kill Brother Wing and Fat Chan, and then shoots himself dead. For Moon, the pistol is a means of destruction and a tool of disempowerment. Chan emphasizes the gulf between Moon's imaginary heroic life and his tragic ending.

Figure 4.3a   Moon has imagined himself to be a brave killer . . .

Figure 4.3b   . . . but he fails his mission and runs away in a panic.

This tragic portrayal of people's fate being tied to a pistol is taken to an extreme in Lam's *The Runaway Pistol*. As noted, Lam was inspired by Chan when they worked together to produce *Made in Hong Kong*. They both share a familiarity with action genre films from working in the industry as assistant directors. Lam's film is highly experimental, personifying the pistol and letting it narrate its own life story from a first-person point of view. Throughout the film, the pistol is passed on from one person to another in an endless journey of tragedy, witnessing the problems commonly associated with broken families and failing relationships. Many echoes are found in this later film where the pistol's symbol of power is not only challenged but also used as a voice of critique of the media and the society at large.

Moon can only have Sylvester, who follows him around. Moon makes some joking remarks that Sylvester is "no Stallone," and "he's most probably the one and only dumb-witted triad member in Hong Kong." Non-heroic characters such as Moon and Sylvester have appeared in traditional Hong Kong gangster movies, but the way in which the directors handle these characters usually cannot intrigue the audience. These kinds of minor characters are not the audience's objects of projection, and cannot make the audience identify with them. Chan, on the contrary, puts these characters under the spotlight. As for Ping, she looks like a common Hong Kong teenage girl. She is definitely not the type of mature or maternal female protagonists in Woo's movies. Yet, Ping has a terminal kidney disease and is dying, so she is still an object of sympathy, similar to the blind nightclub singer (Sally Yeh) in Woo's *The Killer* who needs a hero to save her from a miserable life. While the killer (Chow Yun-fat) in the film has all the characteristics of an ideal hero: intelligent, quick-witted, and ready for self-sacrifice, Moon as the protagonist in *Made in Hong Kong* cannot figure out how to save Ping's life. He has not taken any concrete action to donate his kidney to her to help her overcome her kidney ailment. Ping's death turns out to be partially caused by his ignorance and incompetence.

Compared with the protagonists in gangster movies and even in the *Young and Dangerous* series, they are younger; Ping is only sixteen years old. Being too young and helpless, these abandoned youngsters are not ready to enter the adult world, not to mention take over the older generation's authority. Moon hates the adult world and attempts to confront it, but at the same time he has an emotional attachment to the adults. After his mother has run away, he keeps on trying to catch sight of her around every corner of the city, including the convenience store where she works as a shopkeeper. At the end of the movie, Moon is lying dead in the graveyard, with his voice-over saying, "We die young; we'll remain forever young . . . We're all very happy now. We aren't afraid even if we have to face an uncertain world, because we've been immune." His voice raises doubts about the myth that young people are full of optimism and hope for the future. As Moon, Ping, Sylvester, and Susan die young, there is no need for them to face the uncertain future, and this can be a happy ending for them. Chan's narrative addresses youthful helplessness, rather than youthful power as celebrated in the *Youth and Dangerous* series.

In gangster films, no matter whether the protagonists are gangsters, killers, or cops, they are in one way or another caught up in the state of homelessness. Stephen Chan argues that as *jianghu* signifies a space away from home, one's sense of homelessness is coupled with the spirit of exploration in a world of adventure and danger. It is a dangerous zone but it is not an entirely lawless society which is governed by "its own set of laws, its own code of ethics, and its own social structure."[26] We can find similar signification in the *jianghu* of gangster films.[27] In a discussion of Woo's *A Better Tomorrow* (1986) and *The Killer*, Julian Stringer suggests insightfully that gangster films are very much concerned with the theme of homelessness, which is more historical and cultural than transcendental. He holds the view that while the killer in Jean-Pierre Melville's *Le Samourai* (1967) carries some traits of an existential hero, Woo's heroes express the sense of uprootedness caused by the 1997 handover.[28] Similarly the sense of homelessness in the young gangster films, for example the *Young and Dangerous* series, is also evoked. Stokes and Hoover make a similar point when they analyze the connection between the two types of gangster films:

> The rootlessness of the characters in the series is emphasized by shooting many scenes in Hong Kong streets, with groups of youths, either the handful of featured Hung Hing boys or *en masse*, several hundreds together, always in motion, moving through and moving on. This instability is lamented in a way that evokes the nostalgia evident in Woo's movies. Characters search for roots through substitute fathers and families.[29]

While these motion images of the triad boys in the urban space of Hong Kong were shot on location, in the actual Hong Kong streets, realistic motivations were clearly not the filmmakers' concern. Even the historical reference to a slum fire at the outset of *Young and Dangerous 1* does not pertain to correct factual evidence.[30] As Stokes and Hoover have observed, there is a strong sense of alienation and homelessness. The search for roots at the time of the political transition to 1997 echoes with that in the older gangster with the new element of the search for father from the triad boys. However, these innovative elements appeal less to our sense of the real than to nostalgia. In fact in scenes where hundreds of triad boys cluster in the city, the *mise-en-scène* functions to persuade us to regard it symbolically, to perceive the criminal underworld as a *jianghu*, as a figurative trope. Although the young gangsters are uprooted problem boys from broken families, they are portrayed as heroes who adventure and join in the "race for power and excellence" in the underworld/*jianghu* (fig. 4.4a). They are no longer lonesome, melancholic heroes like Melville's killers but their male bonding is close to those in Woo's heroic gangsters. In addition to brotherhood and loyalty that they uphold, team spirit and collectivism are essential. This shift from individualism to collectivism characterizes the *jianghu*'s mode of heroism, celebrating and romanticizing the power of the new and young. The rootless cruising of hundreds of them in the urban space depicted by freeze frames recycles the spectacle of heroes in the comic book series of *Teddy Boy* (figs. 4.4b–4.4c). Although the film series still celebrates individual heroes such as Ho-nam and Chicken, the vitality of the younger generation lies in their community spirit.

Figure 4.4a *Young and Dangerous 1*: Young gangster leaders, followed by hundreds of triad boys, move along the streets of downtown.

Figure 4.4b The film ends with a spectacular scene . . .

Figure 4.4c   . . . which is subsequently transformed into a comic image.

Etzler's short film *Film 2 HK 1995* is a crude attempt to launch a *détournement* of this generic depiction of the urban space. In order to shatter the cinematic spectacle popularized by the series, in ten minutes' time, the artist simply cuts away all the clips where human beings are seen in *Young and Dangerous 1*. What is left is only a series of quick montage images of Hong Kong's urban space and the soundtrack of the original film. This kind of *détournement* results in the destabilization of meaning in the original film. One may observe that now the city, which is a space without heroes, has become the protagonist. Speed, congestion, violence, and chaos characterize this fast-paced urban space of alienation and homelessness. The fixed meaning evoked by the heroic triad images is displaced. This diversion does not "tell" us another set of meaning but rather "shows" us what the Hong Kong city is like. It then constructs a new text, what Jenks calls "a new synthesis," through the process of deconstruction.[31] The "transtextual" cues in this new text enhance the sense of indeterminacy one often finds in a deconstructive text.

In a different way, *Made in Hong Kong* deconstructs the young gangster series by shattering the triad boys' community spirit. The spectacle of cool boys in freeze frame is now displaced by melancholic, lonesome youngsters who roam the streets of Hong

Kong (fig. 4.5). Moon declares his individualism clearly at the outset of the film:

> I'm a lone-wolf type of person, doing whatever I like to do. To me, freedom counts. I'm unlike other rascals, I've brains. I don't take orders. I won't kill when they told me to risk my life just because that's an order. The most important thing is to equip yourself with skills. This is my style.

However, Moon is not the same as the lonesome killers in *Le Samourai* and *Leon the Professional*, because unlike them, individualism is not his wish. Moon is somewhat socially alienated as he is excluded and rejected from mainstream society. He does not go to school and he cannot find a job; he cannot lead a normal life like his friend, Keung. Above all, he is abandoned by his parents. At the same time, he does not get very involved with the gang members and he has no interest in gaining recognition in the triad society. Stokes and Hoover point out that the *Young and Dangerous* series expresses an urge for "[n]ewness and a fear of being outdated," as one of the characters says, "the world is changing rapidly . . . We have to be updated." Also, the triad boys living in remote districts yearn for a chance to go downtown to have a look at the outside world.[32] However, Moon remains living in a low-cost public housing estate. He wanders around housing estates and old markets, where the lower-middle class, old people, abandoned youth, and kids reside. Being separated from the affluent districts in Hong Kong, these poor areas conjure up a sense of negligence and oblivion. Yet, changes sneak into these relatively static areas, which most inhabitants may find difficult to cope with. There is a scene in which Moon is on his friend's van traveling along an old low-cost housing estate where the sidewalks are under massive re-construction. Facing the continuous renewal of urban space which makes the city unrecognizable and uncanny, Moon suffers from a sense of homelessness, as he replies to his friend, "I've no idea where I'm heading for" (fig. 4.6). Living homeless is not Moon's wish, and he does have a physical home in a public housing estate. The shabby public housing estates in the *Young and Dangerous* series, on the other hand, are romanticized as the breeding grounds for legendary triad heroes, conveying a sense of nostalgia and warmth. However, Chan emphasizes the dark side of these housing estates as dangerous places where murders, killings, and fighting often take place. The neighborhoods respond to these crimes with indifference and coldness, incapable of making any changes to such a terrible living condition. Chan's depiction of these spaces, in particular Moon's home, is deadly. It is abandoned by his father and then by his mother, and eventually, it becomes haunted and deserted.

Figure 4.5   Sylvester, Moon, and Ping watch the students playing on the playground.

Figure 4.6   Moon looks out onto the torn-up sidewalk.

Moon's individualism does not rule out community building in the film. However, if the term "community" connotes stability, regularity, and security, signifying "the desire to have a sense of shared space, orderly and respectful of personal space," the film diverts from it by portraying what I would call "an erotics of the deadly communal."³³ This idea is further explicated in Chapter 6 where I argue that alienation in the film is always encountered with the possibility of community building. When familial relationships are shattered, it is haphazard youthful friendships that generate human connection. The graveyard scene where Moon, Ping, and Sylvester search for Susan's ghost is the most explicit expression of this possibility. The open space of the graveyard is agoraphobic but seductively panoramic. Using a series of panning shots of the countryside, the youngsters are not devoured by open space; instead they trespass the open space, standing on unknown tombs and trying to gain a visual panoramic control of the territory beyond the graveyard (fig. 4.7a). However this community also asserts a form of subjectivity that has enabled a collective bird's eye view of the deadly open space of the countryside (fig. 4.7b). Before this graveyard scene, the characters are seen traveling on a speedy KCR train. Together with an airplane that passes by the open rooftop space where Susan commits suicide, the speedy train suggests that this community of youngsters is continuously subject to social and political mutation of all kinds (figs. 4.8 and 4.9).

The sense of homelessness and rootlessness, derived from the city of alienation, divorces itself from the heroic order of the underworld/*jianghu*. If we can regard *Made in Hong Kong* as a *détournement* of the gangster film, we may argue that it recodes the *jianghu* by way of reinterpreting the meaning of heroism, individualism, and community at a moment of critical transition. Laikwan Pang made an interesting point about Chan's "Handover Trilogy" with regard to this sense of deadliness that is explicated here: "Fruit Chan's 1997 trilogy is one of the few that does not see death simply as an aporia or a new beginning but as means of revealing one's subjectivity...."[34] — a fatal way of allowing oneself to be heard.

Figure 4.7a   The three youngsters try to attain a visual panoramic view of the countryside.

Figure 4.7b   All they can see is a deadly open space.

Figure 4.8   An airplane flying in the background.

Figure 4.9   Moon, Sylvester, and Ping travel on a
train to the countryside.

5

In Search of the Ghostly in Context*

I tried my best to use those housing estates that are unique to Hong Kong to highlight its image — this uniqueness is the whole spirit of *Made in Hong Kong*.

— Fruit Chan[1]

Defamiliarizing the city at a moment of danger

Made in Hong Kong demonstrates a dual moment of defamiliarization. The previous chapter described how realistic motivations were mobilized to shatter the myths and ideologies inherent in the dominant, commercial genre. Realism as a style in Fruit Chan's other films clearly embodies an alternative vision to

---

* Some portions in this chapter have appeared in two of my previous papers, "The City That Haunts" and "Built Space, Cinema, the Ghostly Global City," but the material has been significantly reorganized and new perspectives have also been added.

Hong Kong history and culture depicted in commercial cinema. On the other hand, his "realist" films should be regarded as a mixture of realistic and surrealistic traits. In his "quasi-realist" style, a "spectral city" is constructed.[2] This mixed mode, involving dramatic and surrealistic elements, undermines one's sense of reality at a moment of critical transition. It also shows the state of confusion of a troubling selfhood. If Chan attempts to "write up" an urban historiography of Hong Kong through his films, such "writing up" is also a hermeneutical endeavor to make sense of the changing environment.

Together with *The Longest Summer* and *Little Cheung*, *Made in Hong Kong* conjures up uncanny visions of Hong Kong at a critical moment when "time is out of joint." When Jacques Derrida cites Shakespeare's *Hamlet* to refer to contemporary time as "a time out of joint," he suggests that haunting is an epistemology which enables him to articulate the relation between deconstruction and Marxism in the new world order after the events of 1989.[3] With broader concerns than the spectral return of Marxism, an abundant corpus of literature has emerged in the recent decade to explore how the spectral provides, as Avery Gordon puts it, "a very particular way of knowing what has happened or is happening." She argues that the city can be regarded as a site where ghosts gather; a dense site of history and subjectivity where grieving and remembering are always in conflict with forgetting.[4] In a similar manner, Chan's films explore the sense of anxiety, disorientation, and uncertainty which results from the tug-of-war between memory and forgetting.

We can trace Chan's early interest in the ghostly city before he became independent. *Finale in Blood* (1991/1993), a romantic ghost story, is one of the two films made when he worked in the commercial film industry. The Chinese title of the film literally means "Uproar in Kwong Cheong Lung." It is a famous ghost story and has numerous adaptations in different forms of art. The story originated in Guangzhou, and can be traced to the late nineteenth century. A ghost asks a young scholar to help her to avenge her death. She hides her spirit in an umbrella, so the scholar can bring her to Kwong Cheong Lung, a small hotel where her ex-lover had taken over from her by force. Chan's *Finale in Blood* uses the same plotline, but it is in the radio days of Hong Kong, probably in the pre–Second World War time. With the help of a young radio broadcaster, the ghost Fang Yin (Nonie Tao) tells her tragic love story to the public through a radio program. She is killed the second time in bloodshed in Kwong Cheong Lung, together with her husband and his mistress. The first half of the film echoes Stanley Kwan's *Rouge*, in which the ghost Fleur returns from the underworld and asks a journalist to help look for her lover. Like Fleur in *Rouge*, the figure of Fang Yin looks like a living woman. Sometimes she is visible, sometimes she is invisible. The last scene of the film shows Fang Yin, her husband, and his mistress walking together under an umbrella. The eerie slow motion camerawork captures the ghostly images of the three.

The invocation of the ghostly in Chan's films is not a turn to the literal understanding of specter. The ghostly young girl Susan in *Made in Hong Kong* appears only as recurrent images in the protagonist's dream (fig. 5.1). At other times, when there are disappearing humans who appear ghostly, such as the teenage boy's dying grandmother in *Little Cheung* (fig. 5.2) and the disbanded Chinese soldier in the British army (fig. 5.3), there is no association with the metaphysical genre of the ghost story. It is therefore more precise to talk about the ghostly than the ghost genre. The invocation of the ghostly makes things strange, resulting in the restoration and manifestation of the shock impact of the urban phantasmagoria. If the turn to ghosts, specters, or apparitions offers an instrument of "defamiliarization," or what the Formalists call "*ostranenie*," spectral analysis in this discussion is not a metaphysical exercise. On the contrary, ghostliness, to quote

Gordon again, "draws us affectively against our will . . . into the structure of feeling of a reality" that we can experience "as a transformative recognition."[5] As the Latin etymological root of "specter" indicates, the denotative reference to a ghost, a phantom, or an apparition connotes feelings of fear and dread. "Specter" also derives from the Latin verb "*spectare*," which means to behold, having the same root for "spectator." In this connection, the spectral city as an analytical category requires a careful explication of the problems of visuality in the mundane urban space.

Figure 5.1   *Made in Hong Kong.*

Figure 5.2   *Little Cheung.*

Figure 5.3 *The Longest Summer.*

In the first instance, the spectral city is fundamentally about what can or cannot be seen; about what is half-seen, allegorically seen, or quickly seen, to borrow from Ackbar Abbas's typology of visuality.[6] In the next chapter where I analyze the spectral city in Chan's films, the feeling of estrangement is explored with reference to two major kinds of uncanny city spaces which provoke questions about presence/absence, visibility/invisibility, and appearance/reality. They are the low-cost public housing estates and the old neighborhoods in Hong Kong. These urban spaces, whether they are indoor domestic spaces or outdoor ones, are cinematically represented through the manipulation of light and darkness, warped space, shadows, and abject images, all pertaining to Abbas's idea of what is half seen and allegorically seen. They also contribute to the defamiliarization of a city made too familiar by the global urban landscape of the Victoria Harbor skyline glorifying the notion of modernity-as-progress. As often noted by critics, the skyline of the Victoria Harbor has been articulated in the official discourse as a signifier for Hong Kong's economic success.[7] Its overexposed visibility shapes what critics call the "grand narrative" of Hong Kong while the "petite narratives" (*petit récit*) can only derive from forgotten spaces such as low-cost housing estates and old neighborhoods.

By focusing on what is half seen and allegorically seen, Chan pays specific attention to the state of homelessness arising from such a global city. However, in addition to the banal angst of feeling homeless and rootless in a modern life-world, the trope of the spectral city in his "Handover Trilogy" is not simply an expression of pessimism. These visions, as forms of transformative recognition, open up new, alternative visions of remembering a city in critical transition. As Henri Lefebvre argues, being a subject involves accepting "a role and a function" which implies "a location, a place in society, a position" which we can call "space."[8] Through his films, Chan claims the subject-speaking position to articulate his visions of Hong Kong. By situating his characters in the space of the city, he offers them an opportunity to "recognize for themselves" their right to the city which has forgotten their existences.[9]

The surreal intrusions that are present in Chan remind one of the spectral Paris that stimulated the nineteenth-century French poet Charles Baudelaire's imagination. Baudelaire's poetic image of the swan as a surreal intrusion in the changing space of nineteenth-century Paris evokes strong unsettling feelings. In "The Swan," Baudelaire writes:

> . . .
> Paris changes, but nothing of my melancholy
> Gives way. Foundations, scaffoldings, tackle and blocks,
> And the old suburbs drift off into allegory,
> While my frailest memories take on the weight of rocks.
>
> And so at the Louvre one image weighs me down:
> I think of my great swan, the imbecile strain
> Of his head, noble and foolish as all the exiled,
> Eaten by ceaseless needs — and once again
>
> Of you, Andromache . . . [10]

To the lyric poet in the era of high capitalism, the prototype of the Benjaminian *flâneur*, the swan is a ghostly figure of the past lurking in the contingent, disappearing space of the present. It is a melancholic space traversed by the homeless, the exiled, the widowed, the orphaned, and many more who suffer. Tracing the historical background of the poem, we can see that it was a space transformed by massive modernization projects under Georges Haussmann's "strategic beautification" designs in the mid-nineteenth-century France.[11] Gone was the old Parisian city which, like the suburbs, had turned into allegory. The Parisian city in transition was visualized by the poet-*flâneur* as one haunted by specters of the past and disturbed by the sense of anxiety, disorientation, and uncertainty in the present. The heaviness of memories, like the "weight of rocks," negotiates with the forces of forgetting.

In a similar way, Hong Kong in Chan's "Handover Trilogy" is also frequented by surreal, ghostly intrusions of various kinds. They are the allegorization of recalcitrant elements of the past that resist erasure. The surreal in Chan's films evokes the heavy weight of melancholic sentiment in "The Swan" and reminds us of the ambiguous status of the ghostly subjects. As ghosts always return with a story to tell, the ghostly subjects in Chan's films stubbornly persist in the space of the present that does not want them. Their presence upsets the linear temporal order of modernity, turning the urban space into what I would call a "spectral chronotope." If chronotopes, as Mikhail Bakhtin theorizes, refer to the specific temporal and spatial settings in which stories unfold, spectral chronotopes in films are constructed to express the feeling of loss and disorientation which results from space-time dislocation. This is a topic to which we will return in the next chapter.

Politics, class, and the urban space

The portrayal of Hong Kong as a ghostly space was not a new invention in Hong Kong cinema when Chan's "Handover Trilogy" was made. There has been a long tradition of ghost films in Hong Kong cinema. Surrounding the 1997 handover, quite a number of films drew on the image of the haunted house to refer to the anxiety aroused by the uncertain future. As big box-office successes, the horror films of this era rely quite heavily on special effects to create fear, excitement, and above all, visual pleasure. Sammo Hung's *Vampire* series (1985–88) and Ching Siu-tung's *A Chinese Ghost Story* (1987) are among the most representative. A shared view among critics is that the popular reception and commercial success of this horror genre are symptomatic of anticipation of the onset of 1997.[12] For example, Stephen Teo observes that ghosts, cadavers, monsters, and the like have been allegorized as "apocalyptic portents of disaster."[13] In a similar way, Sek Kei reads such films allegorically, claiming that the "specter of 1997" has transmogrified into ghostly figures that wander the lands of Hong Kong.[14]

The cinematic trope of the haunted house finds its root in the political and cultural reality of the people of Hong Kong. In the mid-1980s when the fate of Hong Kong was sealed in the Joint Declaration of 1984, the image of the "haunted house" could not be divorced from people's anti-communist sentiment. The most blatantly dramatic expression of revulsion toward the Chinese state was the massive exodus of middle- and upper-middle class élites and professionals to other countries in the 1980s and 90s. For some, the main reason for migrating was to preserve their capitalistic way of life — a lifestyle that had been fostered by British colonial hegemony over the years. This exodus was cinematically expressed as the flight from the haunted house. Other films beyond the ghost and horror genre also drew on the trope of the "haunted house." *Swordsman* (1990), a collaborative *wuxia* film by Tsui Hark, Ching

Siu-tung, and King Hu, ends with a memorable panic-stricken and yet comic moment when people disperse in haste, deserting their homely abode without hesitation.

While this allegorical reading of Hong Kong as "an *unheimlich* house" illuminates the Hong Kong–China relation in a specific historical and political context, it tends to downplay the significance of socio-economic background in shaping film texts.[15] In critical discourses on Hong Kong films, not much attention has been paid to the issue of class. Where class is discussed, it is mainly to critique the plight of middle-class people.[16] However, Chan's focus on socially marginalized classes has attracted some critics' attention. As noted in Chapter 1, Natalia Chan Sui-hung and Wimal Dissanayake's essays are some fine examples. To offer something new to this scholarship, I explore the intricate relation between urban space and social marginality by developing strategies of reading the surreal and ghostly elements in Chan's films.

In the critical discourse on spectrality and globality, Fredric Jameson's neo-Marxism informs us with views from political economy. Further developing his earlier works on postmodernism or what he also calls "second modernity," Jameson explores the role of finance capital and land speculation in mediating cultural forms such as architecture in *The Cultural Turn*.[17] He argues that the architectural style of the "second modernity," characterized by "extreme isometric space" and "glass skin," and its "enclosed skin volumes," now produces endless, universal, and dematerialized space which erases the difference between a "brick" and a "balloon."[18] Architectural style is thus sometimes a cultural and ideological smokescreen which is deeply rooted in a society's political economy. He further suggests that there is an intricate relation between postmodern architecture and spectrality. While architecture is the symbol of capital, it is often the very site of finance capital. The realm of residential high-rises in Kwan's *Rouge*, for example, belongs to a modern-day Hong Kong middle-class couple who are naturally involved in contemporary forms of service industry such as journalism and the media. The couple's fascination with the half-self-deceptive story conjured up by the ghost is not unlike the contemporary form of nostalgic consumption. Although the film can be read as a response to the moment of transition in 1997, I resonate with Jameson's view that the haunted residential high-rises are also a metonym of the ghostly global city.[19]

However, there are two important points to note as a critique of Jameson, and in this case, Chan's films serve to illustrate my arguments. First, there is some discrepancy between Hong Kong private high-rises that he refers to in *Rouge* and the postmodern architectural style that Charles Jencks identifies. In fact only the placeless commercial buildings in the business districts satisfy the two characteristics. Although some new private and luxurious high-rises are now equipped with huge windows, a majority of the residential high-rises, whether private or public, are walls and columns of towers without any "glass skin" but only small windows on the building facade. Second, Jameson's spectral analysis is basically anchored in the multi-storey private high-rises which cannot be equated with the massive public housing estates where the majority of lower-middle-class Hong Kong inhabitants are housed. These haunted and haunting living spaces have shaped the mental life of the majority of the population. If private residential housing is a metonym of globalism, public housing estates have a more complex and indirect relationship with the global economy. Spectrality is associated with what is hidden, not known, and nondescript.

To unpack this relationship, we have to first recognize that public housing estates are literally the physical homes of the lower-middle-class people in Hong Kong. *Made in Hong Kong* is a form of self-representation because Chan grew up in one of those estates. *The Longest Summer* also features the public housing estates as homes for culturally marginalized people. There is one scene in which some teenage girls chase after each other along the corridors in Lai Tak Tsuen; they are portrayed as youngsters who cause violence, conflicts, and disturbances in the neighborhood. The disbanded Chinese soldier of the British army, Ga Yin, lives in an old private residential building where the condition of the public space is nearly as unfavorable as that in some old housing estates. He expresses his frustration in his own house at a time when he is not wanted socially and culturally. He shatters the mirror which reflects his split identity at a disjointed time. Class does not seem to be a dominant issue in *The Longest Summer* but any exploration of the condition of marginality cannot be understood without reference to its socio-economic dimension. Although Chan tends either to move to old Chinese apartments (often known as "*tong lau*" in Cantonese) in old neighborhoods or to depict public housing as secret spaces of forbidden trafficking, the images of public housing in Hong Kong have remained central to his portrayal of the plight of Hong Kong's people.[20] He comments on the relation between class and public housing estates in an interview after *Made in Hong Kong* was released:

> Public housing estates are recognizable as what is Hong Kong. In the past, many young people turned into gangsters in areas like Sau Mau Ping and Tze Wan Shan. I have lived under the shadow of the housing estates for a long time. What has lingered in my mind is the dilemma that if I do not leave this place, I will have no prospect at all. The portrayal in *Made in Hong Kong* is in fact a much cleaner version than the one in my memory and experience.[21]

He considers these estates as the representation of the darker side of Hong Kong local culture. *Made in Hong Kong* in fact contains a number of shots depicting the housing estates as prison houses. The barred windows, barb-wired fence of the playground, and the grid-patterned walls of the corridor all foster a *mise-en-scène* of entrapment and imprisonment. While many inhabitants must claim these places as "home," at least as a physical and material home base, the majority of them often lament that their livelihood is far from ideal because of hyper-density, bad sanitation, poverty, dysfunctional families, and neighborhood crimes in these estates. Perhaps the most memorable scene in the film is the shot from Moon's subjective point of view of what is outside his housing estate. It is a partial view of the urban panorama of Sha Tin — one of the new towns where better housing estates were built in the mid-1970s. Moon's view gradually zooms in on two kinds of spaces: the private residential high-rises for well-off people and the transnational Royal Park Hotel along the Shing Mun River (figs. 5.4a–5.4b). At the same time, Moon's voice-over expresses an acute feeling of homelessness:

> I couldn't possibly go home in the next few days. I was sure that Susan's spirit must have been waiting for me. Susan, you'll have to experience the feeling of loneliness. Well, if you can guarantee my safety and refrain from harassing me, I'll be back because this is my home.

如果你能保證我的安全，而你又不再騷擾我的話
Well, if you can guarantee my safety and refrain from harassing me...

Figure 5.4a   The Shing Mun River, a shot from Moon's subjective point of view.

因為這是我的家
Because this is my home.

Figure 5.4b Royal Park Hotel on the left and private residential high-rises on the right.

Home for the youngster has become uncanny because of Susan's haunting spirit. This haunted feeling of homelessness contrasts with the romanticized versions of the housing estates in *The Young and Dangerous* series discussed in Chapter 4. As noted, the fact that reference to the slum fires of 1953 was mistaken as 1956 at the outset of the first film indicates that the gangster films are more concerned with myth than history. The young gangsters return to the housing estates more or less like swordsmen returning home from their exiled experience in the *jianghu*. The housing estates in the young gangster films are therefore positive home spaces which can be escaped to as refuge. They remind viewers who are familiar with Hong Kong television drama series and the New Wave cinema of examples of the housing estates on Hong Kong screens.

Although early television portrayals of public housing estates were used to signify common problems associated with slums, more positive depictions were common in the early episodes of the *Below the Lion Rock* series. For example, in *Dream of Stardom* (1976), the space is crowded but prosperous, and the residents are kind adults and innocent kids.[22] In Allen Fong's *Father and Son* (1981), the public housing estate seems to be a safer living space when compared with the squatter huts. Both the older and younger generations are hard-working, with a desire for upward mobility in the society. For them, the public houses are a transient residency only. Despite their differences, these spaces in the dramas of social realism share some affinity with the ways in which they are valorized in the romantic young gangster films of the 1990s. As Li Cheuk-to suggests, the triad kids are "keen to discover their roots in the public housing estate where they were born or grew up" so that their legendary success as triad society heroes can be affirmed.[23] Whether it is convincing to allegorize the gangster's success as Hong Kong's so-called "miraculous transformation" from a fishing village to a world-class metropolis is one question; nevertheless, to claim one's social roots in these dismal housing estates does not serve so much to critique the pathetic past as to glorify the successful present.

In sharp contrast, the spaces of the public housing in *Made in Hong Kong* and *The Longest Summer* do not affirm this kind of positive signification. As haunted and forsaken places, they evoke ghostliness, melancholia, loss, and nostalgia. When Moon laments that the world is moving too fast, his nostalgic sentiment is not merely social and personal. Allegorically it is better understood in the historical and political context of the handover. The political nature of such a changing space is invoked at the end of the film. When the film shows a collage of replayed and new images presenting the death of the four youngsters, the images intersect ironically with a radio announcer's voice from an imaginary radio station, "People's Radio of Hong Kong," narrating the myth of Hong Kong's reintegration with China and the need to be hopeful about the future. Hope coexists ironically with death as Moon's suicide is portrayed in one of the old housing estates in Hong Kong. These buildings offer poor living conditions for the lower-class inhabitants (fig. 5.5). In this last ironic moment of intersection of image and sound in the film, despair and hope just cancel each other out, depositing a sense of nothingness beyond the limits of words. Although Chan's films are not ghost movies, they share a similar structure of feeling in recent films where the global city of Hong Kong is haunted by a stubborn past. Ann Hui's *Visible Secret* (2001) and Peter Chan's *Three — Going Home* (2002) are two notable examples. The setting of *Three — Going Home* is an old police quarters in Western District, but its structure is very similar to old-style public housing estates.

Figure 5.5   A panning shot across Moon's home, after he has committed suicide at the graveyard.

Earlier history of Hong Kong's public housing

The relationship of this kind of low-cost housing to a sense of homelessness can be further unraveled by examining the history of Hong Kong's housing policy and its socio-economic background. Despite many improvements in government housing in later years, the notorious seven-storey estates found in Shek Kip Mei, Kwun Tong, Kwai Chung, and Lok Fu dominated Hong Kong public housing life for many years. By 2009, nearly all of the buildings in Shek Kip Mei were demolished and redeveloped into newer designs. Except one, all the blocks constructed in the 1950s were vacated and officially demolished by the end of 2006. Block 41 of the estate, named Mei Ho House, is now the last remaining example classified as "Grade 1 historic building" preserved and museumized as a record of Hong Kong's public housing development.[24]

The story of Hong Kong's public housing started with a great slum fire in Shek Kip Mei in 1953. Because of the fire hazards, the Shek Kip Mei Estate was built with the aim primarily to resettle the huge influx of newly arrived refugees from China at the wake of the Communist takeover in 1949. Research has shown that resettlement was not solely motivated by humanitarian reasons. In one colonial government document, the following striking reason is given:

> Squatters are not resettled simply because they need . . . or deserve, hygienic and fireproof homes; they are resettled because the community can no longer afford to carry the fire risk, health risk, and threat to public order and prestige which the squatters represent . . . [25]

Critics are right to point out that after the Shek Kip Mei slum fire, the colonial government's housing policy was more bound up with economic than humanitarian reasons. As Abbas points out, hyperdensity may be perceived as a result of limited space in this small city but, more precisely, the scarcity of land is always exploited for profit-making.[26] Another critic also notices that the earlier resettlement housing estates in fact aimed less at providing welfare than allowing the government to acquire valuable development land and to reproduce cheap labor.[27]

The dismal living conditions and ill-equipped facilities in these housing estates were clearly a result of hasty construction and the government's lack of genuine concern to provide welfare. Although the British colonial government had always adopted a *laissez-faire* strategy of non-intervention in the economic policy, this kind of state intervention in housing then helped the government to participate in global processes of capitalist accumulation. One critic convincingly suggests that housing as an object of production (with exchange value) and consumption (with use value) is also a tool for an entrepreneurial government's promotion of capital accumulation for a powerful minority at the expense of the lower-class majority.[28] In subsequent slum-clearance projects following the 1953 fire, the reason for resettlement was basically economic. As the sole supplier of land, the government could generate huge revenues from urban redevelopment by acquiring slums occupying valuable sites in the central city.[29]

Despite this, critics seldom show us that economism cannot explain what is happening to people's experience with their domestic space. In the early 1970s, the colonial government had to rely on welfare and other measures to re-establish its legitimacy which was threatened by the massive anti-colonial riots in 1967.[30] At the same time, a growing sense of social awareness among Hong Kong inhabitants, especially the second generation who came of age in the 1970s, helped give social movements new momentum. Some activists made documentary films criticizing the dismal condition of public housing. Among them, Ann Hui's television drama "The Bridge" (1978) for the *Below the Lion Rock* series featured housing estates as a site of conflicts between government bureaucracy and residents fighting for better living conditions and social services.

These films offer alternative views to official propaganda which boasted resettlement as the government's achievement in housing.[31] The gradual improvement in living conditions and the design of the built space of public housing since the 1970s illustrate both the need for the authority to consider the interests of the dominated; at the same time we can see how the dominated and the ruled can assert their influence in what Lefebvre calls "the representational space," meaning:

space as directly *lived* through its associated images and symbols, and hence the space of "inhabitants" and "users," but also of some artists and perhaps of those such as a few writers and philosophers, who *describe* and aspire to do more than describe. This is the dominated . . . space which the imagination seeks to change and appropriate. It overlays physical space, making symbolic use of its objects.[32]

The representational space is one that the dominated in society can use to express "their rights to the city." With a few decades apart from the earlier Hong Kong screen productions of public housing estates, Chan's *Made in Hong Kong* offers a similar critique of a society of inequality, updated and intertwined with the imminent experience of the political handover. Cinematic mediation offers a powerful kind of agency where "art can become *praxis* and *poiesis* on a social scale," and we might quote Lefebvre to argue that "the art of living in the city" is a "work of art."[33]

Recent history of Hong Kong's public housing

Placed in the larger context of social history, *Made in Hong Kong* articulates some intriguing moments of homelessness inherent in the housing estates. As Hong Kong's economy escalated in the late 1970s and the real estate market boomed in the 1980s, the city was also widely recognized as a global city. During this time, many of the inhabitants of public housing had been lured into home ownership. While some returned to redeveloped public housing, many improved their living conditions by either participating in the government-funded home ownership scheme or purchasing homes from private investors. This shift was also accompanied by the society's gradual transformation from manufacturing to service and technology industries. As a result, some of the decrepit and abandoned public estates are now homes for members of the lowest stratum of Hong Kong society; among them are the elderly, the under-privileged, and newly arrived immigrants from mainland China.

In Chan's earlier films, these estates are like ghost towns. Although Chan's *Dumplings* has taken a different turn in the portrayal of these estates, he still seems to be preoccupied with associating the housing estates with a sense of ghostliness. In *Made in Hong Kong*, Susan's suicide, which makes her aged parents lonesome and saddened, is also metaphoric of the decrepitude and ghostliness of this space in Hong Kong. We might even say that it is not Susan's ghost that haunts this space but it is this space that has become haunting. The story that this ghostly space tells is far more than just a story of the British colonial government's hasty resettlement, consequently providing an inhuman and unacceptable living environment. It is also a story about the government's long-term negligence of the social and economic condition of the underprivileged. Without doubt, global cities are noted not only for their celebratory features such as the euphoria of networking, prosperity, and technological advancement, but also as sites of social and economic inequality as well as uneven developments.

From minimal intervention in the 1950s to active provisions in later years, the history of colonial housing policy was succeeded by a dramatic turn after 1997. David Harvey observes that the transformation of urban governance in advanced capitalistic countries involved a shift from a managerial approach to entrepreneurial forms of action in the 1970s and 80s.[34] It is believed that an entrepreneurial stance would be beneficial to economic development. In the case of The Hong Kong Special Administrative Region (SAR), the government after the end of British colonialism continued to be dominated by entrepreneurs. During the first few years under Chief Executive Tung Chee-hwa, a former businessman, the government declared its desire to be global, to turn Hong Kong into a world city, and to be on a par with London and New York.

During the late transitional period to 1997, the discourse of modernity-as-progress was constructed on many levels to cope with Hong Kong's inevitable political change. The most notable examples are the grand infrastructural projects such as the new airport initiated even before the last colonial governorship of Chris Patten. Some of these projects were continued after the handover by the SAR government to boost Hong Kong's status as a so-called "world city." On top of the projects associated with the handover, the perpetual process of destruction and construction in the city space is the rule rather than the exception. While Hong Kong aspires to be a world city, many social developments, including housing policy, have continued to be subject to either stasis or chaos. As Chan observes, "The design of public housing is puzzling in that after all these years its provisions are still no more than the most basic living conditions, with little signs of improvement for the general living conditions."[35] So before 1997, despite the grand projects in infrastructure, the speed of change in living conditions was not up to par with other projects of modernization.

The other ironic example would be the SAR government's decision to boost the sense of home-ownership in Hong Kong inhabitants after 1997 so as to establish hegemony and legitimacy.[36] However, the housing plan, which aimed to create 85,000 homes per annum, fell through in a short time because of strong opposition from land developers and real estate investors against government intervention. This more recent example shows clearly that there have been long-term uneven developments in the society of Hong Kong. So while inhabitants of the public housing estates are traumatized by inevitable political and social changes in general and some also have improved their living condition by moving out of their dismal living space, the pervasive sentiments are often associated with stasis and entrapment. Stasis and change in this case are two sides of the same coin. This alarming contradiction seems to suggest that in an era of globalization, the unglamorous and the abject spaces, such as the public housing estates, are not so much juxtaposed against the grand and prosperous global cityscape — the landscape that is celebrated and consumed by political leaders, entrepreneurs, and the like. Rather they exist as the silent accompaniment of this "Significant Other," as the hidden and the repressed in the global city. They are haunting and haunted spaces in the city. Michel Foucault once claimed in "The Eyes of Power" that "the history of spaces" would also be "the history of power."[37] Instead of focusing on the issue of the power of surveillance, I would argue that the history of spaces that we can trace through Chan's films underlines the urgency of writing an alternative history of empowerment at a state of emergency.

Emotion in context

If unprecedented political events and socio-economic developments carry a shock impact on city inhabitants in a period of transition, Chan's films show us an array of responses from those who are socially and culturally marginalized. This reference to the powerless helps us unpack the relation between spatial design and social inequality. At the same time, it highlights the intricate relations among emotion, identity, and historical transformation. Among the current accounts of emotion, the social constructivist view provides a conceptual framework for understanding this relation.[38] Similar to cognitive scholars who maintain that emotions affect the agent's judgment and action, social constructivists concur with the view that emotional states are associated with human intention. However, instead of focusing on the immediate psychological causes, they try to trace the socio-political roots of emotion. The broader orientation of the latter view carries some important implications for understanding collective emotion manifested in *Made in Hong Kong* and *The Longest Summer*. The feeling of homelessness in these films expresses the general troubling problem of selfhood at a moment of crisis but it is also very specific to the lower-middle-class people. Insofar as there is no universal emotion but only culturally specific and diverse forms of emotion, we can claim that the feeling of homelessness in the film enables us to understand the culture of disillusionment and anxiety at a specific historical (dis)juncture in Hong Kong. Mette Hjort and Sue Laver put it very succinctly by saying that "[i]n some instances, social constructivism is a matter of urging a hermeneutic stance designed to ensure that theoretical discussions reflect the self-understandings of the agents whose emotions are under scrutiny." This argument emphasizes the agent's ability to "shape and give meaning to their lives" and therefore any analyses of emotions "become mere impositions of cultural concepts and frameworks."[39] The pursuit of a project in connection with the ghostly city will not be complete without reference to its class dimension and Hong Kong's cultural specificities.

6

In Search of the Ghostly in Urban Spaces*

[T]he ghost is not simply a dead or a missing person, but a social figure, and investigating it can lead to that dense site where history and subjectivity make social life. The way of the ghost is haunting, and haunting is a very particular way of knowing what has happened or is happening.

— Avery Gordon[1]

The spatial uncanny

The notion of the "ghostly city" in Fruit Chan's films is not a literal reference to actual ghosts; the emphasis is more on the exploration of homelessness. With reference to recent scholarship on emotion,

* Some small portions of writing in this chapter have appeared in two of my previous papers, "The City That Haunts" and "Built Space, Cinema, the Ghostly Global City," but the material has been significantly reorganized and new perspectives as well as new analyses have also been added.

the feeling of homelessness in *Made in Hong Kong* can be traced to the 1997 handover and the longer-term socio-economic background of lower-class people and their dismal living conditions in low-cost housing estates. The disbanded soldiers, illegal immigrants, and prostitutes from the mainland depicted in Chan's later films played no part in the grand narrative of Hong Kong as an economic miracle. These characters are also associated with objects of abjection, for example, dirt, filth, and waste matter. They are readily subject to abjection and expulsion in both literal and symbolic senses. Chan himself calls this "low aesthetics," which reminds us of his label of being a "grassroots director." This kind of aesthetics, in Chan's view, is not of "low class" or "bad taste"; it is "created out of everyday life."[2]

While most middle-class inhabitants in Hong Kong would define their everyday life in association with chic shopping malls and consumerism, Chan places his characters of social and cultural marginality in unglamorous city spaces, such as brothel houses, side-street cafes, old neighborhoods, public housing estates, and slums. Some of these spaces are on the verge of disappearance. One of the demolished slums, Tai Hom Village, where *Hollywood Hong Kong* was filmed, now haunts passers-by like a specter. At one point, its rumbles and ruins stood shamelessly opposite to the popular shopping mall called The Plaza Hollywood. Images of the old neighborhoods in Mong Kok, Yau Ma Tei, and Sham Shui Po are also retrieved largely through documentary realism in *Little Cheung*. These forgotten people and spaces re-appear in Chan's cinematic space to make the city spectral. On the other hand, many of them are intriguingly connected with the globalism and tourism. The virtual space of pornography in *Hollywood Hong Kong* and eerie public housing estates of secret trafficking in *Dumplings* demonstrate the invisible and uncanny flows of images and desires. In this chapter, the focus will be on the ghostly interior and the spectral exterior which are two kinds of spectral spaces in *Made in*

Hong Kong. As nearly all his characters in *Made in Hong Kong* are associated with public housing estates, the sense of ghostliness cannot be understood without reference to the experiences of the lower-class people.

Anthony Vidler's *The Architectural Uncanny* and his subsequent work *Warped Space* provide very useful perspectives for the exploration of aspects of the spatial and what he calls "the architectural uncanny," as it has been characterized in literature, philosophy, psychology, and architecture. His focus is not on uncanny architecture, which he argues does not exist; but rather, on "the architectural uncanny." I will modify it by calling it "the spatial uncanny" as both the indoor architectural space and urban exterior are discussed in this present context. It is clear that Vidler's "architectural uncanny" has been informed by Sigmund Freud's oft-quoted notion of the *unheimlich*, but Vidler's appropriation of the term deviates from its original, psychoanalytical context.

From the provocation of the homely, stable, and domestic nature of "home and house" to the general reconsideration of questions of social and individual alienation, exile, and homelessness, Vidler deals with this doubleness with reference to Western intellectual and aesthetic history since the nineteenth century. He provides a historical and theoretical account of the architectural uncanny as cultural and historical representations of estrangement. Vidler's major interest is in urban sensibility, fear, anxiety, and paranoia, and how they are associated with space. In the third part of *The Architectural Uncanny*, the city figures centrally as a site of estrangement, and as *topos* for the exploration of anxiety and paranoia: "[t]he interpretative force of the uncanny has, in turn, been renewed in literature and painting but above all in film, where the traces of its intellectual history have been summoned in the service of an entirely contemporary sensibility."[3]

If architecture is the natural habitat for the uncanny, film is its immediate abode. Walter Benjamin has implied such an interesting link between the medium of film and ghostliness in his seminal essay "The Work of Art in the Age of Mechanical Reproduction." In his nuanced discussion of how new forms of visuality are opened up by new media of his time such as photography and film, he says, "[t]he camera introduces us to unconscious optics as does psychoanalysis to unconscious impulses."[4] If psychoanalysis functions to decode the meanings of hidden impulses, traumatic past experiences which are beyond clear re-telling, and haunted feelings which are symptomatic of another reality, then the film medium is not very different from a psychoanalytic tool. As the camera manipulates various kinds of spatial representations, ghostly beings, all of which have been banished or displaced in the conscious process, are made to reappear as the repressed that return. In *Reflections*, Benjamin articulates more directly the relation between built space and hidden reality by saying that "[c]onstruction fills the role of the unconscious."[5]

Instead of adopting a psychoanalytical approach, this chapter employs a "psycho-social analysis," which focuses on questions of history and aesthetics. Avery Gordon has suggested that "uncanny experiences are haunting experiences," but "the investigation of these qualities of feelings is . . . a more properly aesthetic than psychoanalytic topic of inquiry."[6] Vidler and Benjamin emphasize the relation between spatiality and feeling. The following questions persist: Whose feelings are articulated through such spatial representations? If the "ghostly" is an antidote to mystification in psychoanalysis, can psycho-social analysis help to demystify the social and cultural specificities inherent in the spectral city of Chan's films? On the level of film representation, the sense of ghostliness evoked in film texts can be understood as culturally specific. Viewing film as a meta-discourse, Chan's cinematic depictions of the ghostly city are hermeneutical acts to articulate the experience of the lower-class people at a disjointed time in Hong Kong history. On these two levels of agency through which we can analyze production, representation, and reception, a film spectator sympathetic to the plight of the underprivileged is posited.

Fruit Chan's aesthetics and film style

"The ghostly city" as an aesthetic category aims to evoke the sense of homelessness, dread, and alienation that one feels at a place which is called "home." It carries the same interpretive power as the "architectural uncanny" to trace an unsettling and ambiguous contemporary sensibility produced by urban mutations. Like Vidler's "architectural uncanny," it cannot be confined by a specific medium or the genre of the ghost story. "The ghostly city" in Chan's films is deeply rooted in Hong Kong's unique colonial experience and its postcolonial moment of transition tied with postsocialist and globalizing trends in China and the larger world outside.

As mentioned before, public housing has always been a tool for the entrepreneurial government to accumulate capital for the ruling class at the expense of the lower-class majority. On the level of representation, "the ghostly city" is often repressed and invisible in the global, celebratory discourse. If the glamorous Victoria Harbor skyline with commercial high-rises is constructed as Hong Kong's grand narrative celebrating its miraculous transformation from a fishing village to a world-class metropolis, the anonymous low-cost estates are its repressed or banished other. Like the lower-class, underprivileged people, they are spaces that are forgotten. At other times, when the low-cost estates are re-presented as central images as in the *Below the Lion Rock* series produced by RTHK, they are invoked to serve as a "decorative other" to highlight the Hong Kong collective spirit which has made miraculous transformation possible. It is often implied that this spirit is borne by a hardworking, enduring population, whose social origins can be traced back to these modest, lower-class housing.

"The ghostly city" in Chan's films bears no reference to these two versions of Hong Kong's success stories. It draws our attention to the darker side of reality and how the sense of estrangement can be countered and dealt with. Through the manipulation of "ghostly chronotopes," Chan problematizes the sense of security that one feels in a worldly global city. As colonial modernity interfaces with postsocialism to shape Hong Kong's particular postcolonial experience, the sense of disorientation depicted in his films has not diminished. Mikhail Bakhtin uses the term "chronotopes" to refer to the time-space configurations in literary discourse, suggesting the inseparability of space and time. In his famous, oft-quoted passage, he conceptualizes the idea in the following way:

> In the literary artistic chronotope, spatial and temporal indicators are fused into one carefully thought-out, concrete whole. Time, as it were, thickens, takes on flesh, becomes artistically visible; likewise, space becomes charged and responsive to the movements of time, plot, and history. This intersection of axes and fusion of indicators characterizes the artistic chronotope.[7]

He suggests that specific chronotopes correspond to specific genres, which represent particular world-views. Take the Greek romance novels which were written between the second and sixth centuries AD as examples. Bakhtin calls them the "adventure novels of ordeal," telling the story of how male and female protagonists face the obstacles to their love, their subsequent separations, and their final reunions. To depict their adventures, the characters are placed in a vast, exotic space. Events then unfold by chance without a predictable sense of everydayness. As Pam Morris suggests, "due to the changeless, atemporal and exotic, foreign characteristics of the time/space determinants, the hero lacks any sense of historical becoming. What is positively affirmed by this chronotope is the durability and continuity of human identity."[8]

In a different way, the "ghostly chronotopes" in Chan's films do not represent any universal world-views but rather articulate a specific structure of feeling defined by a sense of dislocation at various changing moments in Hong Kong history. The discordant sense of space-time configuration in the ghostly chronotopes is evoked by three devices: the use of narrative repetition, the manipulation of light and darkness, and the depiction of warped spaces. They provide "parametric devices," generating aesthetic effects.[9] In Chan's films, these parametric devices are the major determinants conveying the sense of dread, melancholia, and estrangement that one sometimes feels in an urban context. These negative feelings evoke a wild cry from the repressed, banished, and silenced for their right to the city. The ghostly city thus enables haunting as an epistemology, drawing us closer to "transformative recognition" after the experience of being haunted.[10]

The ghostly repetitions in Fruit Chan's films

In formalistic analysis, repetition and parallelism are essential principles of film form. These formal repetitions, often known as "motifs," may appear as "an object, a color, a place, a person, a sound, or even a character trait" but they are often repeated with variations.[11] In *Made in Hong Kong*, there are mainly three major types of repetitions which evoke a sense of ghostliness: Susan's haunting, surreal appearance; the spectral return of the inhospitable spaces, both indoor and outdoor; and Moon's ghostly voice-over.

The surreal, ghostly recurrence: spectral temporality

Made in Hong Kong is punctuated by the disturbing recurrence of Susan. Each of her ghostly appearances in the film is unique in its own way, arresting time to move forward and subjecting it to repetition. This kind of ghostly temporality insists on the significance of the past modes of consciousness and experiences. Its persistent and resilient repetitions show that memories can never be completely erased.[12] Similar to the typical ghost-like victim who returns to avenge his or her anger, Susan is often quiet and voiceless. Except in one scene where we hear her voice through her dead letter, she only exists in other people's consciousness, perception, dream, and memory. The mysterious nature of her bluish haunting image lures the characters and the viewers into the journey of the ghostly search.

With apparent documentary realism, the film opens with an unsettling beginning when the viewers hear Moon introducing himself and Sylvester as failing, abandoned youth. Shot on location, the public housing estates and the basketball court cue the viewers to anticipate a realist docu-drama. But immediately afterward, in her blue school uniform, Susan's ghostly, voiceless body appears as a surreal intrusion when she wanders on the rooftop of a Hong Kong high-rise building. According to Chan, the location is Yuen Ngai Street, near Prince Edward Road in Kowloon, Hong Kong. She is situated on a pre-war building with four to five storeys; it is a typical kind of old tenement house, usually called "*tong lau*" in Cantonese. The scene's bluish tone conveys an acute sense of melancholy and dread. When she jumps off from the roof, the deadly, tragic destinies of the four youngsters are connected. We then hear Moon's voice-over saying, "Mom was right in saying that things are predestined." This statement not only foreshadows the youngsters' fate but also acts as a social commentary on the plight of the disaffected. Moon, Sylvester, and Ping later become intrigued by her death, finding out at the end that they all share the same fate of being forgotten, abandoned, and destroyed by irresponsible adults. If the city can be regarded as "the site of our encounter with the other," as Roland Barthes suggests, Moon's subsequent wet dreams and active fantasies in which Susan's ghost recurs illustrate that otherness does not always alienate one individual from another.

In this first instance when a low-angle shot is made, the monumentality of a typical Hong Kong multi-storey building is emphasized. This overwhelming sense of monumentality is intricately tied with agoraphobia and vertigo which are generally felt on rooftops. While this low-angle point of view is introduced by Sylvester, its perception is not limited to him as the camera soon becomes the audience's eyes (fig. 6.1). For an ordinary Hong Kong film spectator who is familiar with this type of suicide story from the rooftops of the high-rise buildings, this opening sad tale connects itself to many other frustrating experiences of living in Hong Kong, where jumping off high-rise buildings has accounted for the majority of the suicide cases.[13] The sense of familiarity associated with the rooftop as a deadly space is inseparable from the negative experience of living in the public housing estates.

Figure 6.1   A low-angle point-of-view shot of Susan.

Some critics have observed that Susan's falling image can be read in the context of a masculinist discourse. Tracing this kind of falling image to Chan's earlier mainstream film *Finale in Blood*,

Long Tin argues that Chan's preference for falling images indicates a kind of panoramic view of the masculinist kind. He notices that in the first instance, when Susan falls, she ends up resting beside Sylvester's feet. Subsequently, the repetition of Susan's falling death in Moon's wet dreams indicates how male sexual desires can be fulfilled by the death of the girl. He then further argues that this kind of male narcissism can be placed within the context of the 1997 handover.[14] Chan's films reveal a world without fathers, just as Hong Kong in transition was also in a fatherless state.[15] This psychoanalytical reading points out the sexual relationship between the characters. Susan's recurrent appearances can be read both as Moon's wet dreams when he is asleep and as his fantasies during masturbations. As the girl's pathetic, deadly fall satisfies Moon in his wet dreams and active fantasies, she is also a victim in her relationship with her teacher who abandons her. If the monumental high-rise building can be read as a phallic symbol of power, as some feminists suggest, the deadly leap does not render any victory but only exposes the male characters in crisis.

While this reading of the crisis of masculinity is suggestive in both its psycho-social and political dimensions, it polarizes the youngsters who are supposed to share the same fate. It is true that the strangeness of ghosts often alienates and frightens those who encounter them; however, Susan is embraced rather than antagonized by the other three youngsters. Ping, Sylvester, and Moon's collective invocation of the girl's spirit in the vast graveyard is an attempt to build up their youthful community after adults from home and school have shattered their hope. One may observe a similar kind of "retribalization" in the *Young and Dangerous* series discussed in Chapter 4 as many young gangsters come from broken families. However, since Moon's community does not celebrate and romanticize the power of youth, the process of retribalization in *Made in Hong Kong* articulates a different possibility of how a self-other relation can be enacted. In Moon's first wet dream, white fluid flows profusely out of Susan's body and it then fantastically mutates into red blood (Figs. 6.2a–6.2b). In the last moment of the film when Moon has just shot himself dead, images of milky white fluid and red blood flowing across the ground appear again. In both cases, surrealistic elements intrude on the film text, eliding the boundary between waking and dreaming, between self and other, between inside and outside. Although the film may sound pessimistic as it deals with the condition of a dead end at a critical time, this transcendence of the boundary between differences suggests that strangeness and foreignness can be coped with. We may even encounter a situation where we confront our strangeness within ourselves, as Julia Kristeva suggests.[16] Although the focus of *Made in Hong Kong* seems to be on localism, this philosophical implication with regard to strangerhood in a cosmopolitan context is illuminating. If the ideal of cosmopolitanism relies on how one is able "to engage with the Other," and to establish "an intellectual and aesthetic stance of openness toward divergent cultural experiences," as Ulf Hannerz puts it, discovering "a stranger" within oneself is the first key to making connection with others.[17] Kristeva is insightful to say that "we must live with different people while relying on our personal moral codes . . . A paradoxical community is emerging, made up of foreigners who are reconciled with themselves to the extent that they recognize themselves as foreigners."[18]

In this light, Chan's vision of how an uncertain future can be faced does not reside in a simplistic celebration of youth power, as the young gangster series implies; he is interested in coping with the emergence of differences at a changing time. Politically, the voice of the radio announcer from "People's Radio of Hong Kong" speaks metaphorically about linguistic and political differences between Hong Kong and China. Interpersonally, Moon's irresponsible father represents the prototype of the Hong Kong man who keeps a mistress. The mistress's accented Cantonese suggests that she might

Figure 6.2a   White fluid flows out of Susan's body.

Figure 6.2b   It then mutates into red blood.

have come from mainland China. Economically, Moon's gangster boss is busily trafficking with his mainland counterparts. The end of the colonial era in 1997 opened up a new age when Hong Kong entered into the political reality of re-integrating with the PRC. It was also the time when the worldwide trend of postsocialism accelerated different kinds of cultural flows between Hong Kong and the PRC, and between Hong Kong and the rest of the world.

In his later films such as *Little Cheung* and *Durian Durian*, Chan further explores this need to come to terms with differences.

Although there is no ghostly figure like Susan in these films, both films deal with the presence of "strangers" in Hong Kong's urban space. They present Hong Kong's urban space as one frequented by the locally born and bred, new immigrants from the PRC, and migrant workers from other parts of Asia. Instead of depicting surreal intrusions like Susan's ghost, *Little Cheung* articulates the urban mutations in Hong Kong by showing us disappearing humans and urban spaces. With the passing of the old world, Fan (Mak Wai-fan), the illegal immigrant from China, has become the "stranger" that Little Cheung (Yiu Yuet-ming) has to cope with. It turns out that the boy feels more estranged with his family than with "strangers" like Fan and his Filipino maid Armi. A similar kind of erosion of the boundary between self and other is highlighted at the outset of *Durian Durian*. The surrealist superimposition of images of Victoria Harbor in Hong Kong and Mudanjiang in Northeastern China parallels the way that one character's voice-over runs into the other in the latter part of the film. As one changing space, Hong Kong opens up into another one, Northeast or Shenzhen; the city and its "strangers" are inevitably brought closer to each other socially, economically, and culturally.

Inhospitable spaces and spectatorship

Preceding the scene of Susan's suicide at the outset of the film, the panning shots of the public housing estates posit a spectator who observes the dwelling space of the lower-class people in the city. This kind of audience identification created by Chan's camera movement brought about widespread resonances when the film was released. As noted, many critics are particularly interested in his depiction of the housing estates. Natalia Chan Sui-hung praises the film's cultural and social significance because of its focus on the negative portrayal of the public housing estates.[19] Another critic,

Bono Lee, remarks in his film review that the film is successful in portraying the sense of entrapment associated with the youngsters' negative experience growing up in the housing estates. Lee is sensitive to how the structural design of the housing estates bears both positive and negative traits. For example, the partition gate for individual dwellings also serves to provide social interactions because it does not block out inhabitants from the public corridor, unlike the door.[20] These local resonances, among others, suggest how the film appeals to local viewers who are familiar with this kind of dwelling. Many viewers might have had first-hand experience growing up in such places.[21]

Agoraphobic outdoor spaces on the rooftop are intriguingly in-between spaces, neither inside nor outside. For congested Hong Kong residents who are often trapped in small residential cubicles, the rooftops have become outlets for them to breathe. Despite their positive function, many films in Hong Kong have represented them as both deadly and ghostly. Ringo Lam's *Esprit D'Amour* (1983), Bryan Chang's *After the Crescent* (1997), and Andrew Lau's *Infernal Affairs 1* are a few examples. The falling images from these high-rises are closely tied with death, no matter whether the cause is suicide or homicide. Considered in conjunction with the domestic spaces which are equally deadly, these in-between spaces of estrangement in a changing city are fundamental to our understanding of the condition of marginality in *Made in Hong Kong*.

One type of public housing in the film is supposed to be Moon's residence where small cubicles are lined on the two sides with a long grim corridor in the middle. Chan remarks that this scene was shot in Lek Yuen in Sha Tin. These corridors are represented as deadly and claustrophobic spaces in the film. Similar to the rooftop, we can say that these spaces are neither inside nor outside. As Vidler puts it, "space is assumed to hide, in its dark recesses and forgotten margins, all the objects of fear and phobia that have returned with such insistency to haunt the imaginations of those who have tried to stake out spaces to protect their health and happiness."[22] Contrary to Le Corbusier's transparent spaces which are constructed to cope with fear and uncertainty by ways of rational grids and circulation of light and air, dark spaces in cinematic representation have been built upon the negative of transparency and visibility to incite fear and to hide.

The shots of the corridor in Moon's residence have some traits of the *film noir* visual style. Both the shots of the corridor and the characters in it are always shown in darkness, illuminated only in part by dim electric lights or natural light from the corridor windows. The film depicts two murders in the gloomy and shadowy corridor. The first murder attempt is a boy being chased by a group of young gangsters. The second one is Moon being stabbed by a young man who is sent by Fat Chan. In both scenes, low-key lighting and dark shadows in the corridor suggest that uncertainty and danger are lurking. Many inhabitants may have autobiographical anecdotes about the feelings of paranoia in these darkened corridors. Death may not always materialize but the constant subjective fear of being followed or attacked at any time has produced many neurotic metropolitan personalities in such dwelling spaces. The darkened space of the corridor in the film not only engulfs death and neighborhood indifference and coldness; together with the instability of the images produced by the hand-held camera, it also enhances the uncertain identity of the killers and the repetitiveness of such stories about youngsters in the public housing. It is also interesting to note that in both scenarios, the darkened corridor is less like a void of death than a tunnel with a dim light and opening on the far end. The light, however, does not seem to signify hope, future, and possibility; it only illuminates the dark — the hidden identity of the gangster who attacks Moon (fig. 6.3). In other words, it does not aim to confirm what is positive and hopeful but to uncover what is hidden. This ambiguity seems to confirm Vidler's point that transparency and light are constructed out of fear of dark spaces that hide and mystify. No wonder in the history of space, "[t]he moment that saw the creation of the first 'considered politics of spaces' based on the scientific concepts of light and infinity also saw, and within the same epistemology, the invention of a spatial phenomenology of darkness."[23]

Figure 6.3   The corridor.

This ambiguous relation between light and darkness brings us to another type of housing which is newer than the previous one. It is where Ping lives with her mother. This is supposed to be an improvement of the previous type with all the cubicles forming a roomy public space in the middle. Some of these housing can be found in Sha Tin and Ho Man Tin. The actual location of Ping's residence was shot in Butterfly Estate in Tuen Mun, one typical peripheral housing estate which is far away from the prosperous central business district. They are more spacious than the previous kinds of housing. However, Chan's depiction of such a space is also deadly. Some psychological studies have shown that schizophrenics are associated with a range of phobias, from agoraphobia to acrophobia to claustrophobia, and how they feel eaten up by space:

To these dispossessed souls, space seems to be a devouring force. Space pursues them, encircles them, digests them in a gigantic phagocytosis. It ends by replacing them. Then the body separates itself from thought, the individual breaks the boundary of his skin and occupies the other side of his senses.[24]

There is a dizzying moment in the film when Moon and Ping are enveloped by the light and space of the open area in an anamorphic shot from the above. As both of them are disfigured, the space of the middle open space is also warped. If dark spaces conceal and frighten, open bright spaces like the courtyard in this kind of estate encircle and devour the inhabitants. In contrast to this agoraphobic space, the interior claustrophobic space of Ping's cubicle is safe, intimate, and erotic where they have their flirtatious encounter, which subsequently develops into a deadly youthful community consisting of Ping, Moon, Sylvester, and Susan.

In Chan's other films, the old tenement house in *Little Cheung* and the housing estate in *Dumplings* are exceptionally depicted as haunted living spaces. In *Little Cheung*, the old tenements are frequented by surreal and ghostly intrusions. There are two surreal moments in the film, and interestingly both moments exist in some form of storytelling. In the first instance, Grandma narrates to Little Cheung the fantastical story of the tenement-house birth of his elder brother Hang who was later expelled by his parents because of his recalcitrant behavior. The second surreal moment arrives after Grandma has passed away. Toward the end of the film, Grandma is half-seen and is vanishing in her old abode. In calmness, she expresses in a ghostly voice her wish to be gone from this complicated world. It is storytelling as a form of a meta-history that restores their forgotten existences in the space of the film narrative. The tenement houses are being subjected to constant erasure by processes of urbanization and modernization, and being appropriated by global capitalistic forces.

The housing estate in *Dumplings* is in Shek Kep Mei. It is the oldest type of public housing in Hong Kong, shabby, poor, and nearly forsaken. The whole estate and its old neighborhood seem isolated from the outside world. The rich colorful interior decoration of Mei's (Bai Ling) apartment in the housing estate is somewhat like an old-style Hong Kong red-light house. In the scenes where Mei is cooking dumplings which are made of mysterious meat, through Chan's *mise-en-scène*, the apartment has an incredibly haunting atmosphere. The rich former star Ching (Miriam Yeung) feels uncomfortable, but the apartment is the site where she, by eating the dumplings, can fulfill her desire of regaining youth and making herself sexually appealing to her husband. However, it is also the site where Mei and Ching's husband (Tony Leung Ka-fai) have a secret affair. The derelict low-cost housing estates in *Dumplings* have become sites of secret trafficking of desire. What alarms the viewers is that the trafficking is done between Hong Kong and a southern city in China where postsocialism has generated cultural flows beyond anyone's control.

The ghostly narrative voice and yearning for community

The use of narrative voice in Chan's films is a prominent formal element which has helped to render a sense of ghostliness. I call this idiosyncratic feature the "ghostly voice" or the *acousmêtre*, following Michel Chion. The *acousmêtre* refers to the image-voice relation in which we do not see the person we hear. It is, as Chion puts it, an "'off screen' voice of someone who has left the image but continues to be there" or one "who is not yet seen, but who remains liable to appear in the visual field at any moment."[25] In *Made in Hong Kong*, Moon's voice-over narrates the whole story without any instability and tension until the last ten minutes of the film. At the beginning, unlike the typical *acousmêtre* whose voice is heard but not seen, Moon is seen together with other youngsters who play basketball in one of Hong Kong's low-cost government housing estates. As the film unfolds, his voice intersperses the narrative more than twenty times, sometimes introducing the characters and their background, sometimes describing his inner feelings to us, at other times commenting on the failing and disappointing adult world. During this process, viewers are led to attach the voice to the youngster's image because it is assumed that the film is simply told from his point of view. However, toward the end of the film when we witness Moon kill himself and his voice continues to linger on, we recognize that the voice that has been speaking to us throughout the film is in fact a dead person's voice.

Admittedly the dead voice that unfolds the story is not a new invention in cinema, but fascinating in this example is how Moon's voice should be heard together with the voices of other youngsters who have also died. The film presents a mixed bag of images and voices: bodiless voices and voiceless bodies which form a community. With the exception of Sylvester who remains a ghostly mute character unable to describe his misery, the suicide letter written by Susan not only contains her final words for her parents but has been co-written and expanded by both Moon and Ping. I have called this "an erotics of the deadly communal" to refer to their erotic relationships with each other. As noted, Barthes has remarked that the city is the site of our encounter with the other; in this instance, what is at issue is not so much urban semiotics but sociality in the city.[26] The youngsters in the film are erotically connected with each other. The collective, ghostly voice in the final scene demonstrates the impossibility of attaching Moon's voice only to his image in a stable manner. His acute expression of homelessness is also shared by other youngsters in the film:

> Ever since my mom left, I've changed some of my habits.
> Whenever I was walking on the street or sitting in a mini-bus, I
> would observe the people around me, hoping to find my mom.
> How I wished she'd suddenly show up in front of me. I know I've
> failed my family, Ms Lee, and those who care about me. But the
> world is moving far too fast, so fast that just when you want to
> adapt yourself to it, it's another brand new world.

The homeless feeling inherent in both tone and content of the above monologue expresses his yearning for his disappearing mother. In his other monologues, he explains why he cannot go home because of Susan's haunting spirit. These speeches echo each other with unease expressing the problems of urban eroticism. This form of sociality is in fact metonymic of the larger youthful alliance consisting of the other youngsters in the film who also come from dysfunctional families. Ping, who is suffering from a terminal illness, has a crush on Moon who also reciprocates; Sylvester, who is abandoned by his family and finally destroyed by the gangsters, is Moon's most intimate friend, having a similar crush on Ping from their first day of encounter. Susan's letter, which finally reaches her parents a long time after her suicide, is a collective testimony by the youngsters who tell their own youthful woes. These four youngsters, sharing the same experience of having grown up in the problematic public housing estates, form a melancholic youthful alliance — an alliance which is deadly and erotic. As mentioned in the previous discussion of Hong Kong public housing estates, the socially and culturally marginalized people and spaces are sacrificed at the expense of Hong Kong's global desire. So the ghostly voices in *Made in Hong Kong* reveal "secrets of class" in the prosperous city of Hong Kong.

In his discussion of the impossible embodiment of the *acousmêtre*, Chion brings to our attention that the term embodiment (*mise-en-corps*) is reminiscent of entombment (*mise en bière*) and interment (*mise en terre*), both of which are associated with death and burial.[27] The *mise-en-scène* of the last scene also evokes this sense of deadliness and impossibility. We see on screen the dead Moon leaning against Ping's tomb, thinking of Susan, Sylvester, Ping, and himself. It is a final moment of the reunion of the bodiless voices and the voiceless bodies. With great irony, Susan's final de-acousmatization (she speaks in the final moment in her letter) parallels Sylvester's re-acousmatization (he is ultimately mute, only reappearing in Moon's memory/ imagination). What naturally follows our discussion here seems to be Gayatri Spivak's famous question: Can the subaltern speak? Can the subaltern enter history and representation? Is their voice an absent song?

The ghostly voice as an aesthetic filmic category forces us to seek the possibility of hearing what we do not see. It is post-traumatic, always produced after the experience but not signifying the end of experience. It is a symptomatic voice which invites interpretation. It is coded with multiple layers of meaning. We may then be tempted to say that this kind of ghostly voice can also be found in other Hong Kong films, such as Wong Kar-wai's *Chungking Express* and *Happy Together* (1997) where voices are sounded out after the fact, narrating a past love story. However, when we examine the material origin of this voice in *Made in Hong Kong*, surprisingly it is deeply associated with the mode of independent filmmaking. According to Chan, this voice is really a ghostly voice which only emerged after an earlier version of the film was made. Chan said, "In the original script, I did not have any voice-over narration, but they were later added to the scenes where the acting was not competent enough."[28] So instead of being an aesthetic category, this symbolic practice where the voice-over is used is in fact the result of having to work with a non-professional cast of actors whose acting did not live up to the filmmaker's expectation. It has become "parametric" when other ghostly elements cohere to depict the sense of dread. This example can be compared to the faded color of the film. While this color tone enhances the sense of deadliness, it is in fact the result of the expired stock-piled short ends of films that Chan gathered in the industry. I argue that the interaction between the material and symbolic practices in this case spells out some basic characteristics of what we call the independent mode of filmmaking.

Countering estrangement: the ghostly as afterlife

Seriality is a characteristic of Chan's films in terms of casting. Sam Lee acts as Ga Suen in *The Longest Summer*, the younger brother of Ga Yin. He plays the role of a triad kid again and kills a man on the beach under a spectacular firework display. Brother Wing from *Made in Hong Kong* plays the same role in the second movie. In *Little Cheung*, the main characters from *Made in Hong Kong* and *The Longest Summer* all appear briefly. Jo Koo acts the role of Little Cheung's brother, Hang's girlfriend. The film ends with the scene in which Little Cheung sees the three youngsters (Moon, Ping, and Sylvester) walking across a zebra crossing; they look very happy. Stopping behind the zebra crossing is a truck; its driver is Tony Ho Wah-chiu who plays Ga Yin in *The Longest Summer*. The scene is read as the finale of Chan's "Handover Trilogy." Fan and her family from *Little Cheung* appear in *Durian Durian*. It is the first part of "Prostitute Trilogy," but some of its materials are taken from the last part of "Handover Trilogy." In *Public Toilet*, Sam Lee is a killer and Jo Koo is her girlfriend. This kind of recycling and seriality of amateur actors might be due to the financial constraints of Chan's mode of filmmaking but is also partly motivated by his intention to create a "signature style." Interestingly, such structural recurrences provoke the viewers who follow his films over the years to enjoy the "pleasure" of his texts, in the Barthesian sense. These recurrences which are not mere repetitions generate multiple meanings. Let us end with one way of reading such ghostly recurrences as the texts' afterlife. The voice, the *acousmêtre*, is an interesting parametric device in his films through which strangerhood and differences can be rethought.

After *Made in Hong Kong*, Chan showed a constant fondness for using voice-over as a parametric device in his films. *Little Cheung*, a story about growing up, is narrated by the male protagonist Little Cheung alternated with Fan's narration. In *Durian Durian*, the same technique is repeatedly used, even more experimentally. Yan the prostitute and Fan the illegal immigrant narrate their different and yet similar experience of time-space dislocation in Hong Kong and at home. Although these two films do not associate the voices with dead people as in *Made in Hong Kong*, the voice used shares the function of depicting a communal one. Despite the characters' different background, they attempt to make connection with each other. The way Little Cheung and Fan bifurcate the narrative space of the film by their narration suggests the diversity of Hong Kong identity. If illegal immigrants from the mainland are often perceived as strangers by Hong Kong people, this use of the narrative voice brings the two parties together. In *Durian Durian*, when Hong Kong and Mudanjiang in Northeastern China are surrealistically merged together as one space, the two voices also fail to attach to the speakers' bodies. Although these voices do not evoke a sense of deadliness as in *Made in Hong Kong*, their bifurcation and coexistence in the film as non-diegetic voice suggest the possibility of countering, if not overcoming, estrangement in Hong Kong's and mainland China's postsocialist urban space. The increased trafficking of people, commodities, ideas, images, and money between the two locales creates more opportunities for "strangers" from the mainland to frequent. Together with migrant workers from other parts of Asia, they shape a new and inescapable situation that the Hong Kong subjects must cope with. As strangers are both far and near, suggested by Georg Simmel more than a century ago, they are sometimes embraced emotionally without physical contiguity. Both *Little Cheung* and *Durian Durian* echo *Made in Hong Kong* in this treatment of the voice as a device to countering strangerhood, if not overcoming it. Of course, when there are escalated cultural flows of all kinds, it is hard to make emotional connection with strangers. *Hollywood Hong Kong* and *Dumplings* both suggest that strangers, who intrude either as sex workers or agents of secret desires, may be physically close but emotionally distant. This difficulty of coping with the conundrum of the phantasmagoric situation between Hong Kong and mainland China results in the creation of exotic and mysterious characters in the above two films. In *Dumplings* when Mei, the secret agent who provides fetuses for food, speaks with her *acousmêtre*, viewers are not only alienated but haunted by a renewed history of the madman-type cannibalism that Lu Xun depicted more than a century ago.[29]

Epilogue:
Grassrooting Cinematic Practices

[A]rt can become *praxis* and *poiesis* on a social scale: the art of living in the city as a work of art.

— Henri Lefebvre[1]

Within a short span of ten years, Fruit Chan has produced an ensemble of films with his own signature style. Motivated by the intention to pursue independence and authenticity, he has shown us how auteurism and creativity have interacted to produce films of immense social and cultural significance. From his energetic and explosive debut to his more quiet docu-dramas, he demonstrates how one's sense of urgency to respond to the changing world renders filmmaking in "a state of emergency," to borrow from Walter Benjamin. Artistic and cultural artifices thrive on threat, danger, crisis, and catastrophe. "As momentous changes in history elicit human responses, their social and historical significance can only be asserted at cathartic moments in history through imaginative and discursive texts of all kinds."[2] Chan's creative-hermeneutical acts are like the German *Erfahrung* which refers to a range of capacities including judgment, evaluation, imagination, memory, and anticipation at a moment of transition.[3] They are both "praxis" and "poiesis," as Henri Lefebvre would describe them.

I call his filmmaking mode a tripartite one elsewhere to refer to his ability to make sense, make strange, and make-do.[4] The value of Chan's films lies in his persistent efforts to make sense of the world through his creative acts, not so much by faithfully recording it but by launching a mixed mode of realism. The quasi-realism depicting the ghostly city in *Made in Hong Kong* has made it one of the best films in Hong Kong New Cinema. It has enabled critics to theorize and contextualize Chan's aesthetics and spatiality in relation to the feeling of homelessness in the Hong Kong experience. Chan's "low aesthetics" inspire such connections with the meaning-production process and the articulation of our society's forgotten experiences.

The generic characteristics and subversion in *Made in Hong Kong* present a film of timeliness, both as a critical response to commercial genre films and as a self-sufficient narrative film. The way in which he makes do between industrial cinema and the personal terrain provokes us to ponder on the possibility of "grassrooting" the world, to modify Manuel Castells's wordings slightly. Chan "grassroots" the world by way of his do-it-yourself model although he is not always alienated from the industry and the mainstream. Grassrooting the space of flows, according to Castells, involves creating pressure from the grassroots, inserting personal meaning by social actors, and developing autonomous expression and purposive horizontal communities.[5] Chan achieved this kind of grassrooting by making do and inspired other filmmakers to follow suit. Like other filmmakers, he has no choice but to go beyond Hong Kong to seek funding from overseas film groups. Like many others, he exhibits his films through international festival venues. He follows the tide but suggests many possibilities through his grassrooting endeavors. As Castells suggests, societies are open to conflictual processes. In a global world dominated by neo-liberal illusion, the construction of alternative meaning always resists the imposition of meaning. Chan and others have demonstrated this perennial, hopeful logic: "Wherever there is domination, there is resistance to alternative meaning."[6] Calling this process a similar name, "globalization from below" or "grassroots globalization," Arjun Appadurai argues that this kind of globalization helps to foster greater democratization and an emancipatory politics through the imagination in social life.[7]

The year 2007 was the tenth anniversary of Hong Kong's handover to China. It was also the year that Chan exhibited his *Xi'an Story* in a few international film festivals. One may also say that his energy and creativity seem to have burnt out as time goes by, especially when the critical *kairos* of 1997 is but a page in history and a few fireworks sparked in the yearly dark summer nights of Hong Kong. But who knows what one can make out of a mundane space of everyday life which is now inseparable from the global space where uncanny, invisible cultural landscapes move across without our realizing them. Social actors situated in such a space will have no choice but to live it, critique it, and transform it. For some, "the art of living the city" is fundamentally "a work of art."

Appendix 1

Interview with Fruit Chan[*]

About Made in Hong Kong

In "Made in Hong Kong: *A Production File*" *released with the VCD, you declared that the film was a "revolution." What did you want to revolutionize?*

I wanted to revolutionize my life. I had been working in the mainstream industry for a long time, but if I had continued conforming to its norms, I wouldn't have shot *Made in Hong Kong*. Suddenly making an independent production is a revolution for each and every filmmaker in the mainstream. Moreover, the content of independent films usually subverts institutions and that's

---

revolutionary to me as well. I couldn't say it's a world revolution, but it's a revolution for my career.

It took a lot of courage to actualize that film. What motivated you to make this decision?

I think it's an accumulation of my experiences in the film industry. In the past, when I heard musicians claim that for them to write good songs, they had to have fallen in love, I didn't believe so. But I soon realized that somehow, it had to be this way. People feel fresh pain each time when they lose something precious, and the lessons that they learn are kept close to their heart. Once they have a chance to actualize these experiences into a piece of work, what they create would be the best, most painful one. Of course, when I shot the film, I didn't realize that these experiences were so valuable to me.

Initially, I didn't have a strong sense of mission. The five of us [the crew] just wanted to make a film, since 1997 was approaching, but no one single film in the mainstream was about the issue. The year 1996 also marked the one hundredth anniversary of cinema. Moreover, the film short-ends that I saved up were almost expired; they would have been wasted if I hadn't used them, so I gave it a shot. I wrote the screenplay of *Made in Hong Kong*, believing that it would give rise to a good film. Of course I didn't anticipate that its impact would be this great. It's like some spiritual forces pushing me to make this film. I just felt that the timing was right and it was my turn. I had turned down many jobs, because I felt a great passion to finish the film — I knew I had to seize the moment — and I didn't care about making money. In the mainstream, once you've got a chance to become an assistant director, you probably stick to it [the mainstream], as it's financially remunerative, but that was not my choice in 1996. Even if the film turned out to be a failure, I could go back to work as an assistant director again.

There are a lot of resistant elements in the film which challenge Hong Kong genre films. Does the film aim to resist and subvert the Young and Dangerous *series?*

Yes. Why? Because the series was a huge box-office hit, but when I analyzed the series from a moral perspective, I found the messages they preached were in fact contaminating. Since the series was a huge box-office hit, I thought people would grow to become this way and so would our society. I once heard a mother calling a radio phone-in program, praising it as a good film. If parents also lacked the ability to decipher the ideology behind this film, our society was at a moment of danger. If I shot a film just like the *Young and Dangerous* series, about a "triad-kid" hero who pretended to be smart and courageous, it would be no different from them. So I decided to destabilize that heroic point of view. Moon ostensibly seemed to be a hero, but in the end he was just a loser. His monologues at the very end of the film were in fact self-reflections, criticizing himself. If I hadn't come across that mother's phone call on the radio, I might have taken up the traditional heroism central to Hong Kong cinema and probably wouldn't have dealt with the issue in such depth. In fact, human beings have both their panicky and non-panicky sides. With gang fights, gangsters can't always slaughter others and might instead be slaughtered themselves. So if we analyze gangsters from a humanistic angle, we'll find they aren't heroic and daring all the time. Once I used this perspective to view Moon, the outcome was different.

Made in Hong Kong *was released in 1997. Was there any political stance?*

Yes, definitely. At the time I made the film, my political awareness wasn't that strong, but truthfully, what lied underneath was something else. This was because before and after the handover, our ways of life and social structures were undergoing tremendous changes. We had grown up in colonial Hong Kong where we enjoyed a certain degree of freedom, but after 1997 we have to live with a government that doesn't care about freedom. This is a big problem that Hong Kong people have to face. It's absolutely true that the film has a political subtext, but it's a matter of whether it is situated in such a context.

The iconic image of Hong Kong housing estates is very prominent in the film. Can you talk about the different locations of where you shot the film? Was Moon's home shot in Wo Che Estate in Sha Tin?

The architectural shape of Wo Che Estate did appear in the scene in which Moon smashed the TV set, but the actual shooting location was in Shun Lee Estate [in Kwun Tong]. We visited many housing estates while shooting the film, like those in Kwun Tong, Sau Mau Ping, and Kwai Chung, but we discovered that they were too old . . . overwhelmingly old. I therefore decided shooting in Lek Yuen [in Sha Tin]. It's the typical kind of housing estate with a long corridor, but relatively cleaner and a bit bigger. The scene in which Moon was stabbed in a corridor was shot there. Susan's home was shot in a housing estate near Lok Fu. The place where she committed suicide was on Yuen Ngai Street, near Prince Edward Road. It's a pre-war building, four- or five-storey high. Ping's house in Butterfly Estate [in Tuen Mun] was chosen because of its typical well-shaped style, the one with a courtyard in the middle. In fact, there's another beautiful housing estate in Tai Hang called Lai Tak Tsuen, the one that's circular in shape, like a public square, where in *The Longest Summer* the gangs were chasing each other around and around. Although I didn't shoot it in *Made in Hong Kong*, I find it's very interesting. I tried my best to use those housing estates that are unique to Hong Kong to highlight its image — this uniqueness is the whole spirit of *Made in Hong Kong*.

Although many film critics labeled you as a realist, in fact you've employed a lot of surrealist techniques in your films, especially in The Longest Summer. *What is your opinion about both comments?*

This issue about realism is what I always argue with critics about. I think I'm not solely a realist as it's implausible to reach the kind of realism that can be seen in Iranian films, or mainland Chinese films. Many directors emphasize that if one wants to be a realist, the best way is to conceal the presence of the camera in their films, but that's just their own point of view. Even in those Italian neo-realist films or in the French New Wave films of the early 1960s, the presence of the camera was very evident, but the only difference was that their stories were more down-to-earth.

My films could be termed as "quasi-realism" or "half realism and half fabricated realism," which could mean that they're "fake realism." But with my films, take *Made in Hong Kong* as an example, how can they be categorized? To be frank, they can't because up to sixty percent of the plot is based on real-life events. The innovative part lies in the use of non-professional actors, which is also a technique employed by neo-realists. Almost all actors in *The Longest Summer* were new, but the film wasn't shot using realist methods — it was actually very cinematic. It's also a bit surrealistic; somehow it's hard to tell what it is. I think *Little Cheung* is closer to realism, but that kind of realism is also fabricated. *Durian Durian* doesn't deliberately show the presence of the camera — it delivers a very natural feeling, but this naturalness can easily make people believe that it's realism. So those veteran film critics get themselves into trouble. They have preconceived notions of what realism and neo-realism is, but using these models of the 1960s to weigh or compare my films makes for inevitable discrepancies. I don't care which "-ism" my films belong to. To me, the most important is that there is "energy" in a film and it appeals to audiences. I think mine and theirs [the neo-realists' films] have different kinds of impact, so I don't object to what the critics have called me, but I don't agree with their point of view.

Let's get into more details with the surrealist techniques employed in Made in Hong Kong. *In the scene in which Susan commits suicide, there is both white and red fluid coming out from her body. Does it have any symbolic meaning?*

That unquestionably has symbolic meaning. It's a film about youth. In most films at the time, what is the greatest privilege of being young? The dissipation of time. We all have been young before, but we weren't self-critical then, and when we get older, it's inappropriate for us to criticize the teenagers. I was then wondering what should be used to represent youth. I insisted on finding a symbolic image or mood which alluded to literature, something descriptive such as red represented menstrual blood of the female, and white represented semen of the male. I'm trying to convert the beauty of literature into my films, and ultimately, literature is symbolic, so many possibilities have been generated. But many times they're misinterpreted as having particular meanings. After all these years, I feel a bit scared and troubled actually and I'm now trying to tread softly in others' worlds.

Critics always say that my films are not realistic, for example, criticizing that the policemen's nervousness in *The Longest Summer* was exaggerated. But if they had been around the Hong Kong Convention and Exhibition Centre on July 1, 1997, they would have known that no grain of sand could get in there. Some critics also thought that *Little Cheung* was a nostalgic film about the 1950s. I think they should walk around old districts like Shanghai Street and To Kwa Wan, and they would then discover that many things haven't changed much over the years. Recently, I saw a little boy riding a bike, delivering milk tea in Happy Valley for his family's cafe. He is a real Little Cheung! I would definitely argue with those who think that my stories don't exist in real life. They live in a very myopic world, but criticize that my world is fictional. That's unjustifiable. Our worlds are intrinsically different and that's where the problems arise.

Made in Hong Kong appears to me as a highly experimental film, for instance, you've played around with theme of eroticism and film languages.

Very often new or young directors play and experiment a lot in their films, but the quality of the outcome varies. The so-called "play" can mean "fancy" or just "plain joking," but mine aims to give life a humorous twist, and that's different. A filmmaker's feature debut is usually very energetic, so there is much gusto in *Made in Hong Kong* and it ends up bursting with vitality. But most of the time the energetic vibes die down after a certain period of time. People might say that I shouldn't shoot this kind of film anymore.

Were there specific elements that you intentionally played around with in your other films?

Cinema is part of the entertainment industry, so if I have to depict a solemn story, I would prefer to say it in a humorous way and in my signature style and the storyline is infused with social consciousness. No one has done this in Hong Kong before, so my films are different from others and that's already something. That's also why the themes of my films are very pessimistic. But sometimes, dealing with this pessimism could be happy, humorous, and absurd, and these feelings are hard to suppress. While I was making films this way, my burden seemed lighter and I would feel more relieved. I haven't tried other means yet, but I think my present way is kind of good, so I'll continue to do it this way for now.

Every time I make a film, I make an effort to go beyond myself and to deal with deeper issues. Otherwise, I would have kept on shooting films like *Durian Durian* for the rest of my life. I saw audiences responding well to *Hollywood Hong Kong* in person, and that amazed me [smile]. I was surprised that they even had a great reaction to *Public Toilet*, which is my lightest film, I think. *Public Toilet* is not an easy film in the sense that it has no central theme and is more loose than my previous films. But I don't think it's a failed piece. It was shot on DV and it was the largest project among all of mine, so I'd already achieved my goal. Only the DV medium could give rise to *Public Toilet*, because it would be too expensive to shoot it on film.

What is your own self-assessment of Made in Hong Kong*? Do you think it plays an important role in Hong Kong cinema?*

I don't think it's so important, but it serves as a great inspiration to youngsters. That is, if you have the ability and you are perceptive, you can do it yourself (DIY), and that's the spirit of independent film. The other thing is that, it's by all means possible to make a film this good — possessing substance — even though it's a story about "triad kids" on the surface. You can make it into something sociological and entertaining, and include your own perspective at the same time. Hong Kong films rarely have sociological relevance, and even if they had, it was as shallow as *Sesame Street*. So you could say that I made a certain degree of impact: it was the one and only time that the label "Made in Hong Kong" was shown to people when the local film market was dwelling in its lowest point. I think this label has become influential since then. Whenever people talk about "Made in Hong Kong," they think of me. This makes me proud, but I don't enjoy being indulged in arrogance. It also had a great impact in mainland China. The insiders there all think that it's impossible for a Hong Kong director to make a film so powerful. The audiences in Taiwan responded to it very well, too. Above all, I have gained a lot of status in Chinese communities, and that has exceeded my expectations. Anyway, *Made in Hong Kong* brought me a lot of things, and in these last years, I've been making films holding onto this label. Even when people ask me to shoot commercials, they want me to maintain the style of *Made in Hong Kong*.

About independent filmmaking

Why did you choose to be an indie filmmaker? What is your own evaluation of what it means to be an indie filmmaker?

It's a coincidence, not a deliberate choice. In 1996 because of the reasons I mentioned above, I made a film [*Made in Hong Kong*] that didn't have anything to do with the mainstream. It happened to be successful. Indie means that I do what I want to do — no one monitors me and I do not need to get consent or comment from others. This spirit is also the spirit of an artist. Hong Kong artists are pitiable because to practice art in the mainstream, they have to win consent from many bosses. I resent this, so I shot *Made in Hong Kong* without much planning. I find that if I can maintain the same standard in each of my films, I can survive and carry on with my work, so I try to keep this up. But on the whole that's very difficult because there's a big problem with the market. I've been working this way for about six years and I'm not sure if I can carry on.

What are the constraints that you face as an indie filmmaker?

If there are, I think it's the problem of distribution. There are many types of indie films out there and mine are quite "watchable" when compared to others. But most audiences have a preconception that indies are art-house films and that they won't understand them anyway, so somehow they're rather reluctant to watch them in cinema. Once they discover that indies can be enjoyable and different from the common films, their minds change a bit. But this change doesn't last long because we don't have famous stars to promote the films for us. As an indie filmmaker, I still hope that the audiences go to cinema to view my films, so I've tried my best to make my films appealing to all ages and classes. But, nowadays most people scarcely go to cinema, so many good films don't sell well . . . quite pathetic, really. Films like ours are even harder to sell. Of course, I can still survive if I keep the budget low enough. The problem is that after I make a film, it's meaningless to me if it cannot go public — I don't want to hide it under the bed [smile].

What kinds of funding source do you have?

I have investments from Japan, France, and Korea. There are many film funds abroad, say, the film festival market in France is large and they'll support us as long as they think our work is great. That is how I've survived up to now. Without such a market, I might not be able to continue with my career. More financial support has been given by the Hong Kong Arts Development Council because in the last few years I have had a certain amount of influence in the media domain abroad. Wong Kar-wai and I are the two local filmmakers who have been spending quite a lot of time hopping around. What was the influence that Hong Kong films used to have abroad? Apart from kung-fu, there wasn't anything else. For Wong and me, together with some other local directors, what we show to the world is our local culture. It's important and worth promoting our culture. Some countries, those in Europe in particular, do not enjoy kung-fu films alone. They consider our post-1997 influence part of Greater China's, but we are still living under "one country, two systems," so they want to know what is happening here. This is why we have to show them the characteristics of Hong Kong. Otherwise, they wouldn't think it's worth buying our films. Our kind of art-house films was hard to sell in the past, but there is market for them in recent years.

I noticed that you have an agency [Golden Network Asia] to take care of you and your films' publicity since your third film Little Cheung. *What is your relationship with this agency?*

This company is different from normal distributors. The normal type buys the copyright to the film and then shows it locally, but mine is different. For example, when I want to apply for sponsorship from a French film fund, this agency helps me to handle the application process and earns money from the service charge. They will then follow up with distribution and promotion. My company [Nicetop Independent] can handle these matters on its own, but sometimes I want to save trouble and to concentrate on filmmaking, so it has a symbiotic relationship with the agency, running things and making money together.

What is your own self-assessment as an independent filmmaker? How do you view this identity?

I don't have any particular feeling about this. But once I have started off walking on this path, I feel that this is a very interesting way because I can express myself in ways I like and I can survive on this! This is what makes me continue to be an independent filmmaker, but it is by no means easy. I haven't labeled myself as an independent filmmaker intentionally. In fact, I want to shoot a mainstream film this year. This makes people in mainland China and Europe amazed, "What? You shoot mainstream film? How come?" They might think I had sacrificed my integrity, but I hadn't. There are actually good films in the mainstream, but they [those who are shocked] make the distinction between mainstream and indie too clear-cut. To be honest, if one gives me a good script, I don't care if it's mainstream or not. I only want to make films that I like. The audiences are very realistic. If my films do not appeal to them, they would desert me, but I desert them before they do — to make a film nothing like what they expect from me.

What is your view about the future of indie films?

I think the best way is to let it develop naturally, as indie is not a grand ideal or utopia. Many indie filmmakers think that if their works are successful, they've got a stepping stone to the mainstream industry, so indie becomes a learning space for them. If someone doesn't have a chance to shoot mainstream film, they go the independent route and film whatever they like. I think this is an easier way to do what they want to do. There is no need to perceive a great conflict between the independent and mainstream industries, as the situation in Hong Kong is different. But the local market of independent films is still small and it's really hard to maintain the market. I hope to hold on to the spirit of indie as long as I can.

About the director

Let's talk about your own interest. Which is your favorite film? Do you think you've been influenced by its style and thematic concerns?

It's hard for me to pinpoint a particular one. I'm a classic film lover and I like all sorts of films which can touch my soul, no matter whether they're artistic or entertaining. I would feel inspired if they're good ones. I guess I'm influenced by them on a subconscious level. But there's no film that has obvious influence on me and I don't follow any form in particular. I use my own way to make every single film and I don't care about style. Sometimes I would design the ways in which I would handle a specific scene before the actual shooting. Take *Durian Durian* as an example, it's pretty obvious that the first half is the very noisy environment of Hong Kong and it becomes calm in the latter half about mainland China. These two parts apparently represent two extremely different worlds. But I took a different approach to shooting *Little Cheung* — I let it develop naturally at some point. I don't like works of intentional style, since stylized films often look "cold," and pretentiously cool. I believe that when we're not too conscious of style, a style will come naturally to us.

Do you think you have any influence on the Hong Kong film industry?

I don't know, but I think I have greater influence on youngsters. I've shown to them that we can now use a DV camcorder to shoot films, a practice that's much easier than the days of holding [large] cameras. I'm not sure about my influence right now, although I had rather great influence a couple of years ago. But you know, people are absent-minded and not everyone can follow in my footsteps. I do understand that this film industry should be headed by the mainstream because the general audiences like watching mainstream films. I also understand that public culture is led by stars and that they are commodities. If we don't have films with stars, the crisis that comes after would be extremely large.

What do you think of your reception both local and overseas?

I don't see any difference between the two. I think the most important thing of a film is its appeal to audiences. The audiences are very realistic. If they find a film enjoyable, they would admire the filmmaker's skill in turning a simple story into something richly textured. The local audiences like to watch films from abroad as these films give them sensations different from local ones. Nevertheless, in my films there are many touching moments. My goal is to move people's hearts and I believe there must be things which can captivate those "flesh and blood" viewers. I also try to think of a way to make people get into my films. For example, if I only shot the first half of *Durian Durian*, telling how the young woman from mainland China became a prostitute in Hong Kong, the ending would be plainly instructive. But, do prostitutes have their own thoughts? So in the latter half, the pace slows down, showing what she thinks and how people view her. This part has sublimated the film; it is not just another exotic gaze. I believe every thoughtful thing would create resonance among the audiences. *Made in Hong Kong* and *Little Cheung* have such an impact, too.

Of course, Europeans might feel a little bit confused as they are not familiar with Hong Kong. But there are certain feelings that people share universally, no matter they are from China, Asia, or Western countries. *Hollywood Hong Kong* created pretty much the same reactions in the film festivals in Venice and Korea. Although the audiences there didn't understand our language, they felt interested in the film's visual images. The reaction from local viewers of course was greater as they knew the slang. This is a matter of cultural difference. But if we explained the film to overseas viewers briefly, they would then understand.

Among all your works, which one do you like best?

I like *Little Cheung* a little bit better because it has my childhood memories and indeed, it can manage to capture the bittersweet emotions of childhood. Of course, I couldn't say I don't like *Made in Hong Kong* since it is the first turning point in my life. It has the most vigorous vitality among all my works, but I think I need not explore every subject matter with this same degree of vitality.

I filmed *Durian Durian* in a relaxed manner, but it turned out to be the most well received film of mine. *Hollywood Hong Kong* sums up all the black humor of my previous work. *Public Toilet* talks about life and death — I don't agree with critics that these are big subjects that only "masters" can tackle. Actually, my films are all about growing up and if young people take a close look at my work, they'll find something they like as these films are about them.

What kinds of film style have you established? What are you own film poetics and aesthetics?

My work certainly has its own aesthetics. Many people say that I'm a "grassroots director," that I specialize in shooting films about the marginalized. My films indeed have a kind of "low aesthetics" — it doesn't mean low-class or bad taste, but aesthetics that are created out of everyday life. Some find it easy, some find it hard. It depends on whether or not the filmmaker is fully engaged in that particular type of environment. This is my area of strength in the meantime, but I won't keep unchanged in every piece of my work.

Most of the endings in your films are heartrending and quite pessimistic, like in Made in Hong Kong, *where all the lead characters are dead in the end. Do you think there is any way out for the marginalized?*

At the time I shot *Made in Hong Kong*, I hadn't started to think about the issue of a way out, and it's true that there is hardly any in that film. But there is hope in *The Longest Summer*, which is "to forget the past and start again." *Little Cheung* is a film about the problem of cherishing. People usually don't cherish their things until they lose them, and there is an unconscious hint of the 1997 issue in this regard. *Durian Durian* tells the homeward bound experience of the female protagonist, and when all her schoolmates leave home to make money, she starts to re-think about her life.

This kind of re-appraisal is what Hong Kong people need as it may bring us a way out. In *Hollywood Hong Kong* the lead characters move away happily from their old homes and begin their lives again in a new place. They face great changes, yet they can find their way out on their own.

Appendix 2

Funding Sources and Awards

Title	Funding Sources	Production Companies	Box office in Hong Kong [1]	Awards & Participation in Film Festivals

Made in Hong Kong (1997)	HK$500,000 from friends and family	Nicetop Independent Team Work Production House	HK$1,917,330	• Cinema Novo Film Festival 1997
				    Best Film
				    Best Director
				• Gijon International Film Festival 1997
				    Grand Prix Asturias — Best Feature Film
				    Best Script
				• The 3rd Golden Bauhinia Awards 1997
				    Best Film
				    Best Director
				• The 34th Golden Horse Awards 1997
				    Best Director
				    Best Original Screenplay
				• The 17th Hong Kong Film Awards 1997
				    Best Film
				    Best Director
				    Best New Performer (Sam Lee)

				• Hong Kong Film Critics Society Awards 1998
				    Best Director
				    Recommended film
				• The 50th Locarno International Film Festival 1997
				    Special Jury Prize
				    European Arthouse Confederation Award
				• Montreal International Festival of New Cinema & New Media 1998
				• Nantes Three Continents Festival 1997
				    Grand Prix
				    Young Audience Award
				• Pia Film Festival
				• The 2nd Pusan International Film Festival 1997
				    FIPRESCI Award
				    New Currents Award — Special Mention
				• San Diego International Film Festival 1999
				• Vancouver International Film Festival 1997

The Longest Summer (1998)	Andy Lau and Team Work Production House	Nicetop Independent Team Work Production House	HK$2,180,387	• The 49th Berlin Film Festival 1999
				    Forum — In competition
				• Brisbane International Film Festival 1999
				• Copenhagen International Film Festival
				• Gijon International Film Festival 1998
				• Hong Kong Film Critics Society Awards 1998
				    Recommended film
				• International Film Festival Rotterdam 2000
				• Ljubljana International Film Festival 1999
				• London Film Festival 1999
				• Melbourne International Film Festival 1999
				• Pia Film Festival
				• Slovenia Film Festival
				• Stockholm International Film Festival 1999
				• Udine Incontri Cinema 1999
				• Vancouver International Film Festival 1999
				• Vienna International Film Festival 1999
				    Standard Readers' Jury Award

Little Cheung (1999)	NHK Enterprise 21 Inc. Pusan Promotion Plan Award United Color of Benetton (post-production sponsor)	Golden Network Asia NHK Enterprise 21 Inc. Nicetop Independent	HK$455,968	• Gijon International Film Festival 2000　　Best Art Director (Chris Wong) • The 37th Golden Horse Awards 2000　　Best Screenplay　　Best New Performer (Yiu Yuet-ming) • Hong Kong Film Critics Society Awards 1999　　Recommended film • International Film Festival Rotterdam 2001 • The 53rd Locarno International Film Festival 2000　　Silver Leopard　　C.I.C.A.E. Award — Special Mention • The 3rd NHK Asian Film Festival 1999 • London Film Festival 2000 • The 4th Pusan International Film Festival 1999　　Pusan Promotion Plan Award
Durian Durian (2000)	Wild Bunch (France)	Golden Network Asia Nicetop Independent Wild Bunch	HK$523,015	• The 20th Hong Kong Film Awards 2000　　Best Screenplay　　Best New Artist (Qin Hailu) • Hong Kong Film Critics Society Awards　　Best Film　　Best Actress (Qin Hailu) • The 24th Hong Kong International Film Festival 2000 – Closing film • The 6th Golden Bauhinia Awards 2001　　Best Screenplay　　Best Actress (Qin Hailu) • The 38th Golden Horse Award 2001　　Best Film　　Best Script　　Best New Performer (Qin Hailu)　　Best Actress (Qin Hailu) • International Film Festival Rotterdam 2001 • London Film Festival 2000 • Toronto International Film Festival 2000 • Venice Film Festival 2000　　Golden Lion — In competition

Hollywood Hong Kong (2001)	Self-financed HK$500,000	France Movement Pictures Golden Network Asia Golden Scene Japan Hakuhodo Inc. Media Suits Nicetop Independent UK Capital Films	HK$466,521	• Auckland Film Festival 2002
				• Cinemanila International Film Festival 2002
				  NETPAC Award
				• The 39th Golden Horse Award 2002
				  Best Director
				  Best Costume & Makeup Design
				  Best Sound Effects
				• Hong Kong Film Critics Society Awards 2002
				  Best Screenplay
				  Recommended film
				• The 26th Hong Kong International Film Festival 2002 – Opening film
				• London Film Festival 2001
				• The 6th Pusan International Film Festival 2001
				• Rio de Janeiro International Film Festival 2002
				• Sundance Film Festival 2002
				• Vancouver Asian Film Festival 2002
				• The 58th Venice Film Festival 2001
				  Golden Lion — In competition
				• The 4th Cinemanila International Film Festival 2002
				  NETPAC Award for Best Asian Film

Public Toilet (2002)	Digital NEGA (Korea)	Digital NEGA (Korea) KTB Entertainment (Korea) Golden Network Asia Nicetop Independent	HK$54,024	• Barcelona International Film Festival 2003 • Filmfest Hamburg 2002 • Films from the South Festival, Osolo 2002 • Flanders International Film Festival 2002 • Gijon International Film Festival 2002 • Hong Kong Film Critics Society Awards 2003 Recommended film • Hong Kong Independent Film Festival 2003 • The 27th Hong Kong International Film Festival 2003 • International Film Festival Rotterdam 2003 • Istanbul International Film Festival 2003

				• Kaohsiung Film Festival 2002
				    Kaohsiung Film Critics Associates Award
				• London Film Festival 2002
				• The 7th Pusan International Film Festival 2002
				• Split International Festival of New Film 2003
				    FIPRESCI Award
				• Stockholm International Film Festival 2002
				• Toronto International Film Festival 2002
				• Vancouver International Film Festival 2002
				• The 59th Venice Film Festival 2002
				    ControCorrente (Upstream) — Special Mention
				• Viennale 2002
				• Vladivostok International Film Festival 2003

Dumplings (2004)	Local	Applause Pictures	HK$5,904,355	• Berlin Film Festival 2005
				    Panorama — In competition
				• Brisbane International Film Festival 2005
				• Edinburgh International Film Festival 2005
				• Helsinki International Film Festival 2005
				• Hong Kong Film Critics Society Awards 2004
				    Recommended Film
				• Melbourne International Film Festival 2005
				• Raindance Film Festival 2005 — Closing film
				• San Francisco International Asian American Film Festival 2005

Xi'an Story (2006) (short film)	Mainland China	Zhongbo Media	N.A.	• The 5th Asiana International Short Film Festival 2007, Seoul • The 31st Hong Kong International Film Festival 2007 • The 9th Taipei Film Festival

Notes

Chapter 1   Introduction: History beyond the Death Trips

1   Frank Kermode, *The Sense of an Ending: Studies in the Theory of Fiction*, 31.

2   The names that are used in the book follow those that appear in the English subtitles of the film. Those that appear in the brackets indicate the *pinyin* and Cantonese transcription respectively.

3   See "Interview with Fruit Chan" in Appendix 1 of this book.

4   The term "the cruel tragedy of the youth" comes from Nagisa Oshima's famous film *Cruel Story of Youth* made in 1960. Fruit Chan admits that Oshima is one of his important influences from international cinema. See Chapter 3 for details.

5   See "*Made in Hong Kong*: A Production File," VCD (in Cantonese), produced by Nicetop Independent and Team Work Production House (Hong Kong: Shu Kei's Creative Workshop, 2001).

6   "The New Hong Kong Cinema" that I refer to here draws on the claim made by the Series General Editors of "The New Hong Kong Cinema Series": "The New Hong Kong Cinema came into existence under very

special circumstances, during a period of social and political crisis resulting in a change of cultural paradigms. Such critical moments have produced the cinematic achievements of the early Soviet cinema, neorealism, the 'nouvelle vague,' and the German cinema in the 1970s and, we can now say, the New Hong Kong Cinema" (from the Series Preface).

7   Walter Benjamin, "Theses on the Philosophy of History," in *Illuminations*, 255.

8   See Chapter 2 for more on Lam Wah-chuen, whose *The Runaway Pistol* (2002) was inspired by his collaboration with Chan when they produced *Made in Hong Kong*. See Xiao Bai, "The Indie's Search for Space within the Commercial Institution" (in Chinese); and Bryan Chang, "Independent Mediations," in *The Age of Independents: New Asian Film and Video*, ed. Bobo Lee.

9   See Appendix 2 of this book for details.

10   Miriam Hansen, foreword to Oskar Negt and Alexander Kluge, *Public Sphere and Experience: Toward an Analysis of the Bourgeois and Proletarian Public Sphere*, xiv.

11   See Natalia Chan Sui-hung, "The Cruel Tragedy of Youth: On Fruit Chan's *Made in Hong Kong*," in *Cinedossier*, trans. Doris Li-wen Chang; Yau Ka-fai, "3rdness: Filming, Changing, Thinking Hong Kong"; and Bono Lee, "*Made in Hong Kong* and the Experience of Public Housing Estates" (in Chinese). *Made in Hong Kong* is often praised for its close attention to what is most local.

12   Manuel Castells, "Grassrooting the Space of Flows," in *Internationalizing Cultural Studies: An Anthology*, ed. Ackbar Abbas and John Nguyet Erni, 630.

13   See Appendix 1, "Interview with Fruit Chan."

14   US$1 equals HK$7.8.

15   In "*Made in Hong Kong*: A Production File," Fruit Chan expresses his preference for this sense of authenticity associated with amateur actors.

16   Fruit Chan received financial support from film fund associations in Japan, Korea, and France. See Appendix 2 of this book.

17   People often mistake *Public Toilet* as the third piece of the "Prostitute Trilogy," but in fact the trilogy is still incomplete.

18 See Emanuel Levy, *Cinema of Outsiders: The Rise of American Independent Film*; Greg Merritt, *Celluloid Mavericks: The History of American Independent Film*; and Esther M. K. Cheung, "Dialogues with Critics on Chinese Independent Cinemas."

19 See Peter Wollen, "The Auteur Theory," in *Film Theory and Criticism: Introductory Readings*, ed. Leo Braudy and Marshall Cohen.

20 See Appendix 1: "Interview with Fruit Chan."

21 Wendy Gan, *Fruit Chan's Durian Durian*, 25–41.

22 Tony Rayns, "Made in Hong Kong," 48.

23 See Gan's view.

24 Ackbar Abbas, *Hong Kong: Culture and the Politics of Disappearance*, 33.

25 See Appendix 1: "Interview with Fruit Chan."

26 Timothy Corrigan, "The Commerce of Auteurism: Coppola, Kluge, Ruiz," in *A Cinema without Walls: Movies and Culture after Vietnam*, 104.

27 See Audrey Yue, "*In the Mood for Love*: Intersections of Hong Kong Modernity," in *Chinese Films in Focus: 25 New Takes*, ed. Chris Berry.

28 See Chapter 4 for references to their films.

29 Law Kar, "An Overview of Hong Kong's New Wave Cinema," in *At Full Speed: Hong Kong Cinema in a Borderless World*, ed. Esther C. M. Yau, 32.

30 See Lam Keeto's short comment on *Little Cheung* on Hong Kong Film Critics Society Homepage (in Chinese), http://www.filmcritics.org.hk/big5/?mod=articles&task=show_item&cat_id=0144&item_id=00000353 (accessed August 31, 2004).

31 Chan, "The Cruel Tragedy of Youth," 80.

32 Chan, "The Cruel Tragedy of Youth," 77.

33 Chan, "The Cruel Tragedy of Youth," 80.

34 Wimal Dissanayake, "The Class Imaginary in Fruit Chan's Films."

35 See Yau Ka-fai's abstract to "Cinema 3: Towards a 'Minor Hong Kong Cinema'."

36 Yau, "Cinema 3," 560.

37 Laikwan Pang, "Death and Hong Kong Cinema," 19.

38 Pang, "Death and Hong Kong Cinema," 22.

39 Shu-mei Shih, "After National Allegory," in *Visuality and Identity: Sinophone Articulations across the Pacific*, 149.

Chapter 2   Authenticity and Independence

1   This is sometimes included as the subtitle of Jean-Paul Sartre's major work *Being and Nothingness: An Essay on Phenomenological Ontology*. See also Esther M. K. Cheung's claim: "[l]imited independence is our ontological condition" in "*Durian Durian*: Defamiliarisation of the 'Real'," in *Chinese Films in Focus II*, ed. Chris Berry.

2   Bryan Chang, "Independent Meditations," in *The Age of Independents: New Asian Film and Video*, ed. Bobo Lee, 31.

3   May Fung, "i-Generations: A Tentative Study" (in Chinese), in *i-Generations: Independent, Experimental and Alternative Creations from the 60s to Now*, ed. Hong Kong Film Archive; Connie Lam, "Hong Kong Independent Scene in the 90s," in *The Age of Independents*, ed. Lee.

4   See Fung, "i-Generations," 5.

5   Fung, "i-Generations," 5.

6   See Lam, "Hong Kong Independent Scene in the 90s," 4.

7   See Fung, "i-Generations," 4.

8   See Law Kar, "The Significance of *The Arch*," in *A Comparative Study of Post-War Mandarin and Cantonese Cinema: The Films of Zhu Shilin, Qin Jian and Other Directors*. For a comprehensive study of Tang Shu-shuen, see Yau Ching, *Filming Margins: Tang Shu Shuen, a Forgotten Hong Kong Woman Director*.

9   See n18 in Chapter 1.

10   Stuart Klawans et al., "Round Table: Independence in the Cinema."

11   Greg Merritt, *Celluloid Mavericks: The History of American Independent Film*.

12   Chuck Kleinhans, "Independent Features: Hopes and Dreams," in *The New American Cinema*, ed. Jon Lewis, 308.

13   Chang, "Independent Meditations," 31.

14   Long Tin, "Is There Independence after Entering the Mainstream?" *The 28th Hong Kong International Film Festival: Festival News*, no. 2 (2004), http://www.hkiff.org.hk/hkiff28/eng/info/fn25.html (accessed August 31, 2004).

15   Sam Ho, "The Hong Kong Indie: New Times, New Art."

16   Yau Ka-fai, "3rdness: Filming, Changing, Thinking Hong Kong."

17 See Gan's classification in *Fruit Chan's Durian Durian*, 18–20.

18 Gan, *Fruit Chan's Durian Durian*, 19. See also Cheuk Pak-tong's discussion of the New Wave Cinema through which Gan derives her generalization.

19 See Elise McCredie, "Clara Law: An Impression of Permanence," http://www.realtimearts.net/rt43/mccredie.html (accessed June 30, 2004).

20 Raymond Williams, *Marxism and Literature*.

21 Edmond Pang, Carol Lai, Barbara Wong, and Wong Ching-po are cases in point. These young filmmakers have all produced experimental pieces before making their industrial debut.

22 See Esther M. K. Cheung, "Introduction: Cinema and the City at a Moment of Danger," in *Between Home and World: A Reader in Hong Kong Cinema*, ed. Cheung and Chu.

23 Williams, *Marxism and Literature*.

24 Appendix 1: "Interview with Fruit Chan."

25 See Chang, "Independent Meditations," 30.

26 See Ho, "The Hong Kong Indie," 9.

27 See Cheung, "*Durian Durian*."

28 Tony Rayns, "Made in Hong Kong," 48.

29 Michel de Certeau, *The Practice of Everyday Life*, 30.

30 It took the Best Screenplay prize and Qin Hailu won as Best New Artist at the 20th Hong Kong Film Awards.

31 Sources of these rare archives come from Fruit Chan's agent at Nicetop Independent.

32 See Audrey Yue, "*In the Mood for Love*: Intersections of Hong Kong Modernity," in *Chinese Films in Focus: 25 New Takes*, ed. Chris Berry.

33 See Xiao Bai, "The Indie's Search for Space within the Commercial Institution," 36–38.

34 Alexander Horwath, "Hong Kong International Film Festival 2000," http://www.fipresci.org/festivals/text/hkah. html (accessed August 31, 2004).

35 See Esther M. K. Cheung, "The City That Haunts: The Uncanny in Fruit Chan's *Made in Hong Kong*," in *Between Home and World*, ed. Cheung and Chu.

36 Charles Taylor, "The Politics of Recognition," in *Multiculturalism: Examining the Politics of Recognition*, ed. Amy Gutmann.

37   Mette Hjort, "Danish Cinema and the Politics of Recognition," in *Post-theory: Reconstructing Film Studies*, ed. David Bordwell and Noel Carroll.

38   This assertion may be at odds with the postmodernist view that identity is "made" rather than "given"; while there is no room for this debate at length in this context, what needs to be stressed here is the filmmaker's intention and motivation to be "true" to himself. It is hard to verify one's motives and intentions but it can be generally observed that authentic self-expressions are valued by many indie filmmakers. Such discursive practices always translate into action and deeds even when some of them are seeking financial support from the industry.

39   *Bugis Street* (1995), a film about the transvestites and transsexual prostitutes in Singapore's red-light district in the 1960s, enabled Yonfan to attract greater international attention. His subsequent films, *Bishonen — Beauty* (1998), *Peony Pavilion* (2001), and *Color Blossoms* (2004), show an obsession for sexuality, homosexuality, and eroticism. Fruit Chan worked with Yonfan in writing *Bugis Street* and in producing *Color Blossoms*.

40   See Michael Warner, "Publics and Counterpublics," 56n3, 57.

41   See Appendix 2 for a list of overseas film festivals in which Chan's films have been screened and circulated.

42   Mette Hjort and Scott MacKenzie, eds., "Dogma 95 Manifesto and Its Progeny," in *Purity and Provocation: Dogma 95*, 199.

Chapter 3   There Are Many Ways to Be Realistic

1   Victor Shklovsky, quoted in Kristin Thompson, *Breaking the Glass Armor: Neoformalist Film Analysis*, 197.

2   Thompson, *Breaking the Glass Armor*, 16, 198.

3   Thompson, *Breaking the Glass Armor*, 200.

4   Thompson, *Breaking the Glass Armor*, 198.

5   See Appendix 1: "Interview with Fruit Chan."

6   Li Cheuk-to, "*Young and Dangerous* and the 1997 Deadline," in *Hong Kong Panorama 96-97*, ed. Hong Kong Urban Council, 10.

7   See Wendy Gan, *Fruit Chan's Durian Durian*; and Wendy Kan, "The Real Hong Kong: Fruit Chan Captures the Wrenching Transition of the Ex-British Colony," *Time Asia*, March 8, 1999, http://www-cgi.cnn.com/ASIANOW/time/asia/magazine/1999/990308/fruit1.html (accessed August 31, 2007).

8   Bono Lee, "Fruit Chan's Style" (in Chinese), *Hong Kong Economic Times*, January 13, 2000, Music and Culture section; Esther M. K. Cheung, "*Durian Durian*: Defamiliarisation of the 'Real'," in *Chinese Films in Focus II*, ed. Chris Berry; and Li Zhanpeng, "The Absurd Fruit Chan" (in Chinese), *Macao Daily News*, February 25, 2004, Literary supplement.

9   Appendix 1: "Interview with Fruit Chan."

10   My translation. Author unknown, "DV is Free: Dialogues with Jia Zhangke on Film in a Digitalized Era" (in Chinese), *Let's DV*, http://video.sina.com.cn/dv/2005-09-09/140610700.html (accessed August 31, 2007).

11   Michael Berry, "Jia Zhangke: Capturing a Transforming Reality," in *Speaking in Images: Interviews with Contemporary Chinese Filmmakers*, 192.

12   Sandra Shih, "TIDF Documents 129 Versions of Reality," *Taiwan Journal*, November 17, 2006, http://taiwanjournal.nat.gov.tw/ct.asp?xItem=23486&CtNode=118 (accessed August 31, 2007).

13   See Cheung, "*Durian Durian*."

14   See Chapter 2 in this book where "independent filmmaking" is discussed in relation to Charles Taylor's idea of the moral dimension of the self.

15   Chris Berry and Mary Farquhar, "Realist Modes: Melodrama, Modernity, and Home," in *China on Screen: Cinema and Nation*, 77.

16   Stephen Teo, *Hong Kong Cinema: The Extra Dimensions*, 138.

17   Teo, *Hong Kong Cinema*, 138.

18   See Robin Gatto and Nassim Maoui, "Fruit Chan: The Career Interview," in *FilmFestivals.com*, August 29–September 8, 2002, http://www.filmfestivals.com/cgi-bin/fest_content/festivals.pl?debug=&channelbar=&fest=venice&page=read &partner=generic &year=2002&lang=en&text_id=23127 (accessed August 31, 2007).

19   See Laikwan Pang, *Building a New China in Cinema: The Chinese Left-Wing Cinema Movement, 1932–1937*; Zhang Yingjin, *Chinese National Cinema*; and Berry and Farquhar, *China on Screen*, on different modes of realism in Chinese cinema.

20   See Ng Ho, "The Confessions of a Film Anarchist," in *Hong Kong New Wave: Twenty Years After*, ed. Provisional Urban Council.

21   Literary and filmic examples include Zhao Zifan's *Halfway Down* (1953), Li Kuang's *North Light* (1953), Sima Changfeng's *Spring in Northern Country* (1959), and *Home, Sweet Home* (1950, dir. Yueh Feng).

22   Zhang Zhen, "Building on the Ruins: The Exploration of New Urban Cinema of the 1990s," in *The First Guangzhou Triennial: Reinterpretation: A Decade of Experimental Chinese Art (1999–2000)*, ed. Wu Hung et al., 113.

23   Marshall Berman, *All That Is Solid Melts into Air: The Experience of Modernity*, 15.

Chapter 4   The Art of *Détournement*

1   Guy Debord, *The Society of the Spectacle*, 133.

2   Together with the concepts of *derive* and the spectacle, *détournement* comes from the Situationist International. See Ken Knabb, ed., *Situationist International: Anthology*, 50.

3   Debord, *The Society of the Spectacle*, 144.

4   Debord, *The Society of the Spectacle*, 145–46.

5   Chris Jenks, "Watching Your Step: The History and Practice of the *Flâneur*," in *Visual Culture*, ed. Stephen Jenks, 154.

6   See Meaghan Morris, "Transnational Imagination in Action Cinema: Hong Kong and the Making of a Global Popular Culture," 182.

7   Thompson, *Breaking the Glass Armor*, 18.

8   Thompson, *Breaking the Glass Armor*, 19.

9   The series includes *Young and Dangerous 1* (1996), *Young and Dangerous 2* (1996), *Young and Dangerous 3* (1996), *Young and Dangerous 4* (1997), *Young and Dangerous 5* (1998), *Young and Dangerous: The Prequel* (1998), and *Young and Dangerous 6: Born*

to be King (2000). The first three parts had a box office of around HK$63.1 million in total. However, the popularity of the series did not last long. Its last part had a box office of only HK$7.7 million.

10   Examples include *The Storm Riders* (1998), *Dance of a Dream* (2001), *Infernal Affairs* (2002), and *Initial D* (2005).

11   See the description in the jacket cover of the video. Artists who participated in this project include Nose Chan, Leung Chi-wo, Art Jones, Ellen Pau, Olive Leung, Sara Wong Chi-hang, tamshui:\, and Mathias Woo. *Star City* was curated by Elaine Ng and produced by Nose Chan.

12   Lisa Odham Stokes and Michael Hoover, *City on Fire: Hong Kong Cinema*, 81.

13   See Greg Urban, *Metaculture: How Culture Moves through the World*, 260–65.

14   See discussion in Chapter 2.

15   Wimal Dissanayake, *Wong Kar-wai's Ashes of Time*, 94.

16   Dissanayake, *Wong Kar-wai's Ashes of Time*, 95.

17   Dissanayake, *Wong Kar-wai's Ashes of Time*, 84.

18   Stephen Ching-kiu Chan, "Figures of Hope and the Filmic Imaginary of *Jianghu* in Contemporary Hong Kong Cinema," in *Between Home and World*, ed. Cheung and Chu, 304.

19   Examples include King Hu's *Dragon Inn* (1967) and *A Touch of Zen* (1970), Chang Cheh's *One Armed-Swordsman* (1967) and *Blood Brothers* (1973), Tsui Hark's *The Butterfly Murders* (1979) and *Zu: Warriors from the Magic Mountain* (1983), and Ching Siu-tung's *Duel to the Death* (1983), *A Chinese Ghost Story* (1987), and *Swordsman 2* (1992).

20   The more recent examples of turning the *jianghu* into a political allegory are Johnnie To's *Election 1* (2005) and *Election 2* (2006).

21   Li Cheuk-to, "*Young and Dangerous* and the 1997 Deadline," 10.

22   My translation. The theme song "I can take charge" is sung by the rock group Wind Fire Sea. Its group members, Jordan Chan, Michael Tse, and Jason Chu, play the roles of Chan Ho-nam's comrades in the series.

23   John G. Cawelti, "The Concept of Formula in the Study of Popular Literature," 389.

24   David Bordwell and Kristin Thompson, *Film Art: An Introduction*, 86.

25   The translation is taken from the English subtitle in the film.

26   Ng Ho, quoted in Stephen Ching-kiu Chan, "Figures of Hope and the Filmic Imaginary of *Jianghu* in Contemporary Hong Kong Cinema," in *Between Home and World*, ed. Cheung and Chu, 303.

27   The protagonists in gangster films who are in a state of homeless include young Ho-nam (Nicholas Tse) in *Young and Dangerous: The Prequel*, Dagger (Francis Ng) in Cha Chuen-yee's *Once Upon a Time in Triad Society 2*, Kau (Lau Ching-wan) and Matt (Francis Ng) in Wai Ka-fei's *Too Many Ways to Be No. 1* (1997), and perhaps the most typical of all are the hitmen in Johnnie To's *Exiled* (2006), just to name a few.

28   See Julian Stringer, "'Your Tender Smiles Give Me Strength': Paradigms of Masculinity in John Woo's *A Better Tomorrow* and *The Killer*," in *Between Home and World*, ed. Cheung and Chu.

29   Stokes and Hoover, *City on Fire*, 82.

30   It is stated in the film that 1956 was the year when the slum fire happened, but the correct year of this major fire in Hong Kong's history is 1953.

31   Jenks, "Watching Your Step," 154.

32   Stokes and Hoover, *City on Fire*, 82.

33   Graham B. McBeath and Stephen A. Webb, "Cities, Subjectivity and Cyberspace," in *Imagining Cities: Scripts, Signs, Memory*, ed. Sallie Westwood and John Williams, 252.

34   Laikwan Pang, "Death and Hong Kong Cinema," 28.

Chapter 5   In Search of the Ghostly in Context

1   See Appendix 1 in this book.

2   See Esther M. K. Cheung, "*Durian Durian*: Defamiliarisation of the 'Real'."

3   Terms such as "ghosts," "specters," "haunting," and "hauntology" have entered into critical vocabulary of cultural and urban studies. A genre of spectrality in critical literature is in the making with the general

aim of coming to grips with the new world order after the events of 1989. One of the most notable contributions of course is Derrida's *The Specters of Marx*, which provides an important critique of this new world order that proclaims the death of Marx and Marxism.

4   Avery F. Gordon, *Ghostly Matters: Haunting and the Sociological Imagination*, 8.

5   Gordon, *Ghostly Matters*, 3.

6   Ackbar Abbas, *Hong Kong: Culture and the Politics of Disappearance*, 76–79.

7   See Esther M. K. Cheung, "The Hi/Stories of Hong Kong"; and Ho-fung Hung, "Rediscovering the Rural in Hong Kong's History: Tankas, Hakkas, Puntis and Immigrant Farmers under Colonialism."

8   Henri Lefebvre, *The Production of Space*, 182–83.

9   Lefebvre, *The Production of Space*, 35.

10   Charles Baudelaire, "The Swan," translated by Anthony Hecht, in *The Flowers of Evil*, ed. Marthiel and Jackson Mathews, 110.

11   See Marshall Berman, *All That Is Solid Melts into Air*.

12   See Li Cheuk-to, "Introduction," in *Phantoms of the Hong Kong Cinema*, 9. He suggests what I would call a "socio-psychoanalysis" of the Hong Kong cinema. He argues that there is a "coincidence of the Horror genre's resurgence with the territory's preoccupation with its future and the question of China taking over control in 1997 . . . Since 1982, the Hong Kong cinema had produced on average, a total of ten Horror films per year."

13   Stephen Teo, *Hong Kong Cinema*, 229.

14   Sek Kei, "The Wandering Spook," in *Phantoms of the Hong Kong Cinema*, ed. Urban Council, 13.

15   The notion of the "uncanny" comes from Sigmund Freud's explication of male neurotic fear. The source of his argument is based on the double semantic of the *unheimlich* which is the German term for "the uncanny." As the uncanny involves what is unfamiliar and hidden at the same time, it incites fear, dread, and homelessness when *what is familiar returns as the unfamiliar*. If "the uncanny" refers to what is frightening and what arouses dread and horror, Hong Kong in the 1980s and 90s can be described as "an *unheimlich* house" — a haunted house. To extend the Freudian uncanny to the collective psychical

condition of a people, we can see a striking parallel between repression and colonization. In the case of the people who either fled from their home or those who stayed and felt haunted, the "return" of the Chinese sovereignty was frightening. "Chineseness" — which at this historical juncture can be deciphered as a merging of nation and state — was both familiar and unfamiliar at the same time. If repression is the banishment of thoughts and impulses that conflict with the superego, colonial and capitalist modernity has in fact created a *habitus* for the people of Hong Kong. Although a total process of de-sinicization has never happened in Hong Kong, the possible "onset" of a communist regime even with the "Chinese" label would be unimaginable and haunting.

16   See *City on Fire* by Lisa Odham Stokes and Michael Hoover for their adoption of the Marxist approach in the analysis of film and its mode of production. See Stephen Chan, "Figures of Hope and the Filmic Imaginary of *Jianghu*"; and Blanche Wing-ki Chu, "The Ambivalence of History: Nostalgia Films as Meta-Narratives in the Post-colonial Context," in *Between Home and World*, ed. Cheung and Chu, for the discussions of the middle-class people's search for the status quo during the transition to 1997.

17   Fredric Jameson, *The Cultural Turn: Selected Writings on the Postmodern, 1983–1998*.

18   See Jameson's chapter titled "The Brick and the Balloon: Architecture, Idealism and Land Speculation," in *The Cultural Turn*. His views on "the second modernity" come from Charles Jencks.

19   See Rey Chow, "A Souvenir of Love," in *Ethics after Idealism: Theory, Culture, Ethnicity, Reading*; Leung Ping-kwan's chapter on nostalgia films in *Hong Kong Culture* (in Chinese); Blanche Wing-ki Chu's M. Phil thesis titled *The Representation of Space in Hong Kong Nostalgia Films*, Chapter 2; and Abbas, *Hong Kong*. See also Natalia Chan Sui-hung, "Rewriting History: Hong Kong Nostalgia Cinema and Its Social Practice," in *The Cinema of Hong Kong: History, Arts, Identity*, ed. Poshek Fu and David Desser, for a discussion of other nostalgia films and a similar argument.

20   See *Little Cheung, Durian Durian, Hollywood Hong Kong* for the former, and *Dumplings* for the latter.

21 My translation. Susanna T., "No Future! No Future! Fruit Chan Speaks about *Made in Hong Kong*," in *Hong Kong Panorama 97–98*, 54.

22 Refer to Yim Ho's *Social Worker, Episode 3* (1977), the ending of which suggests that young people are unavoidably influenced by the unfavorable living environment. Such a theme is also common in the early New Wave films about youth crime. The public housing is imagined as a residential area populated by broken families, prostitutes, triad society members, and drug takers. Among these residents are the rebellious or materialistic young people who are prone to committing crimes. Another example is Alex Cheung's *Man on the Brink* in which the public housing estate is like "a hell on earth," to quote from Ng Ho, "The Confessions of a Film Anarchist," 56. Other examples are Cha Chuen-yee's *The Rapist* and *Red to Kill* (both in 1994) focusing on rape cases, and Jeff Lau's *Out of the Dark* (1995) depicting public housing as a haunted and desolated space.

23 See Li Cheuk-to, "*Young and Dangerous* and the 1997 Deadline," 10.

24 See http://en.wikipedia.org/wiki/Shek_Kip_Mei_Estate for pictures of the seven-storey blocks and Mei Ho House (accessed August 31, 2007).

25 D. W. Drakakis-Smith, *High Society: Housing Provision in Metropolitan Hong Kong 1954 to 1979: A Jubilee Critique*, 44.

26 Abbas, *Hong Kong*, 86.

27 See Drakakis-Smith, *High Society*, 44; and John K. Keung, "Government Intervention and Housing Policy in Hong Kong: A Structural Analysis."

28 Ludmilla Kwitko, *Local Manifestations and Global Linkages: The Political Economy of Public Housing in Hong Kong.*

29 Keung, "Government Intervention and Housing Policy in Hong Kong."

30 This legitimacy crisis associated with events in mainland China during the Cultural Revolution had coincidentally turned the MacLehose era into a period during which a kind of "home at Hong Kong mentality" was nourished.

31 See Lui Tai-lok, "Home at Hong Kong," in *Changes in Hong Kong Society through Cinema* for a detailed discussion of "home at Hong Kong mentality" and the contested views of housing expressed by government and pressure group documentaries.

32   Lefebvre, *The Production of Space*, 39.

33   Henri Lefebvre, *Writings on Cities*, 173.

34   David Harvey, "From Managerialism to Entrepreneurialism: The Transformation in Urban Governance in Late Capitalism," in *The City Cultures Reader*, ed. Malcolm Miles et al.

35   Susanna T., "No Future! No Future!" trans. Haymann Lau, 57.

36   See *Chief Executive's Policy Address 1998* and *The Hong Kong Housing Society Annual Report 1998*. The following quotation is taken from the latter, "As Hong Kong prospers, our citizens' rising standard of living has prompted a keen desire for home ownership," 69.

37   Michel Foucault, "The Eye of Power," in *Power/Knowledge: Selected Interviews and Other Writings, 1972–1977*, ed. Colin Gordon.

38   See Mette Hjort and Sue Laver's critical introduction to their edited volume *Emotion and the Arts* for a very clear account of the differences and similarities between the cognitivist and the social constructivist views of emotion.

39   Hjort and Laver, *Emotion and the Arts*, 8–9.

Chapter 6   In Search of the Ghostly in Urban Spaces

1   See Avery F. Gordon, *Ghostly Matters: Haunting and the Sociological Imagination*, 8.

2   See Appendix 1 for the interview. Although it is in a very difficult context, C. T. Hsia's view on "low culture" in traditional Chinese literature is comparable. See C. T. Hsia, *The Classic Chinese Novel: A Critical Introduction*.

3   Anthony Vidler, *The Architectural Uncanny: Essays in the Modern Unhomely*, 10.

4   Walter Benjamin, "The Work of Art in the Age of Mechanical Reproduction," in *Illuminations*, ed. Hannah Arendt, 237.

5   Walter Benjamin, *Reflections: Essays, Aphorisms, Autobiographical Writings*, ed. Peter Demetz, 147.

6   Gordon, *Ghostly Matters*, 50.

7   See Pam Morris, ed., *The Bakhtin Reader: Selected Writings of Bakhtin, Medvedev, and Voloshinov*, 184.

8   Morris, Editor's notes, *The Bakhtin Reader*, 181.

9   See Kristin Thompson, *Breaking the Glass Armor*; and David Bordwell, *Narration in the Fiction Film*. They have noticed that in narrative films certain devices such as color, camera movement, and sonic motifs will become "parameters" when they are repeatedly used.

10   See Gordon, *Ghostly Matters*, 8.

11   David Bordwell and Kristin Thompson, *Film Art: An Introduction*, 66.

12   See Bliss Cua Lim, "Spectral Times: The Ghost Film as Historical Allegory," 292, 299.

13   In a statistical report on suicide cases in Hong Kong in 2006, out of 1187 cases, 614 people killed themselves by jumping off the rooftop. See Suicide Prevention Service, http://www.sps.org.hk/sps_stat.htm (accessed August 31, 2007).

14   Long Tin, *Post-1997 and Hong Kong Cinema* (in Chinese), 137–39.

15   See also Natalia Sui-hung Chan, "The Cruel Tragedy of Youth: On Fruit Chan's *Made in Hong Kong*," because Long Tin derives the idea of the fatherless youngsters from her.

16   Julia Kristeva, *Strangers to Ourselves*, 195.

17   Ulf Hannerz, "Cosmopolitans and Locals in World Culture," in *Global Culture: Nationalism, Globalization, and Modernity*, ed. Mike Featherstone, 239.

18   Kristeva, *Strangers to Ourselves*, 195.

19   Chan, "The Cruel Tragedy of Youth," 78–79.

20   Bono Lee, "*Made in Hong Kong* and the Experience of Public Housing Estates" (in Chinese), 54.

21   My own previous work on the representations of the housing estates in *Made in Hong Kong* can be tied to my own childhood experience of growing up in one of these housing estates.

22   Vidler, *The Architectural Uncanny*, 167.

23   Vidler, *The Architectural Uncanny*, 169.

24   Roger Caillois, quoted in Vidler, *The Architectural Uncanny*, 174.

25   Michel Chion, *The Voice in Cinema*, 4, 21.

26   See Roland Barthes, "Semiology and Urbanism," in *The Semiotic Challenge*.

27   Chion, *The Voice in Cinema*, 140.

28   Susanna T., "No Future! No Future!" 57.
29   This connection with Lu Xun was inspired by Professor Lu Tonglin's talk on Chan's *Dumplings* at the University of Hong Kong. The talk titled "New 'Diary of Madman' in the Era of Global Capitalism" was delivered on June 5, 2007.

Chapter 7   Epilogue: Grassrooting Cinematic Practices

1   Henri Lefebvre, *Writings on Cities*, 173.
2   See Esther M. K. Cheung, "Introduction: Cinema and the City at a Moment of Danger," in *Between Home and World*, ed. Cheung and Chu, 250.
3   Miriam Hansen, Foreword to Oskar Negt and Alexander Kluge, *Public Sphere and Experience: Toward an Analysis of the Bourgeois and Proletarian Public Sphere*, xvii.
4   See Esther M. K. Cheung, "*Durian Durian*: Defamiliarisation of the 'Real'," in *Chinese Films in Focus II*, ed. Chris Berry.
5   Manuel Castells, "Grassrooting the Space of Flows," in *Internationalizing Cultural Studies: An Anthology*, ed. Ackbar Abbas and John Nguyet Erni, 630.
6   Castells, "Grassrooting the Space of Flows," 629.
7   Arjun Appadurai, "Grassroots Globalization and the Research Imagination," in *The Anthropology of Politics: A Reader in Ethnography, Theory, and Critique*, ed. Joan Vincent, 272, 274.

Appendix 2   Funding Sources and Awards

1   Figures from Hong Kong Film Archive.

Credits

Made in Hong Kong / Xianggang zhizao (香港製造)

Hong Kong 1997

Director
Fruit Chan

Producers
Andy Lau Tak-wah
Doris Yang Ziming

Screenplay
Fruit Chan

Cinematographers
O Sing-pui
Lam Wah-chuen

Editor
Tin Sam-fat

Art Director
Ma Ka-kwan

Music
Lam Wah-chuen

Production Companies
Nicetop Independent
Team Work Production House

Chief Production Manager
Lau Kwok-wai

Production Manager
Chan Wai-yeung

Executive Producer
Andy Lau Tak-wah

Line Producer
Yu Wai-kwok

Sound Recording
Yung Chi-chung

Costumes
Tin Muk

Cast

Sam Lee Chan-sam (李燦森)	as To Chung-chau, "Moon" (屠中秋)
Neiky Yim Hui-chi (嚴栩慈)	as Lam Yuk-ping, "Ping" (林玉屏)
Wenbers Li Tung-chuen (李棟泉)	as Ah Lung, "Sylvester" (阿龍)
Amy Tam Ka-chuen (譚嘉荃)	as Hui Bo-san, "Susan" (許寶珊)

Carol Lam Kit-fong (林杰芳)   as Ping's mother (屏母)
Doris Chow Yan-wah (周燕華)   as Moon's mother (秋母)
Siu-chung (小鐘)   as Ms Lee (李小姐)
Roger Wu Wai-chung (胡慧沖)   as Keung (雞仔強)
Chan Tat-yee (陳達義)   as Fat Chan (肥陳)
Chan Sang (陳生)   as Cheung Siu-wing, "Brother Wing"
                                (榮少)

Duration
108 minutes

Color

Language: In Cantonese with Chinese and English subtitles

Bibliography

Abbas, Ackbar. *Hong Kong: Culture and the Politics of Disappearance.* Hong Kong: Hong Kong University Press, 1997.

Appadurai, Arjun. "Grassroots Globalization and the Research Imagination." In *The Anthropology of Politics: A Reader in Ethnography, Theory, and Critique,* edited by Joan Vincent, 271–84. Malden, MA: Blackwell Publishing, 2002.

Barthes, Roland. "Semiology and Urbanism." In *The Semiotic Challenge,* translated by Richard Howard, 191–201. Berkeley: University of California Press, 1994.

Baudelaire, Charles. *The Flowers of Evil.* Edited by Marthiel and Jackson Mathews. New York: New Directions, 1989.

Benjamin, Walter. *Illuminations.* Edited by Hannah Arendt, translated by Harry Zohn. New York: Schocken Books, 1969.

———. *Reflections: Essays, Aphorisms, Autobiographical Writings.* Edited by Peter Demetz, translated by Edmund Jephcott. New York: Schocken Books, 1978.

Berman, Marshall. *All That Is Solid Melts into Air: The Experience of Modernity.* London and New York: Verso, 1982.

Berry, Chris, and Mary Farquhar. *China on Screen: Cinema and Nation.* Hong Kong: Hong Kong University Press, 2006.

Berry, Michael. *Speaking in Images: Interviews with Contemporary Chinese Filmmakers.* New York: Columbia University Press, 2005.

Bordwell, David. *Narration in the Fiction Film.* London: Methuen, 1985.

Bordwell, David, and Kristin Thompson. *Film Art: An Introduction.* New York: McGraw-Hill, 2008.

Castells, Manuel. "Grassrooting the Space of Flows." In *Internationalizing Cultural Studies: An Anthology,* edited by Ackbar Abbas and John Nguyet Erni, 627–36. Malden, MA: Blackwell Publishing, 2005.

Cawelti, John G. "The Concept of Formula in the Study of Popular Literature." *Journal of Popular Culture* 3, no. 3 (1969): 381–90.

Chan, Natalia Sui-hung. "The Cruel Tragedy of Youth: On Fruit Chan's *Made in Hong Kong.*" In *Cinedossier: The 34th Golden Horse Award-Winning Films,* 77–81. Taipei: Golden Horse Film Festival, 1998.

———. "Rewriting History: Hong Kong Nostalgia Cinema and Its Social Practice." In *The Cinema of Hong Kong: History, Arts, Identity,* edited by Poshek Fu and David Desser, 252–72. Cambridge: Cambridge University Press, 2000.

Chan, Stephen Ching-kiu. "Figures of Hope and the Filmic Imaginary of *Jianghu* in Contemporary Hong Kong Cinema." In *Between Home and World,* edited by Cheung and Chu, 297–330.

Chang, Bryan. "Independent Meditations." In *The Age of Independents: New Asian Film and Video,* edited by Bobo Lee, 30–31. Hong Kong: Leisure and Cultural Services Department and Hong Kong Arts Centre, 2000.

Cheung, Esther M. K. "Built Space, Cinema, and the Ghostly Global City." *The International Journal of the Humanities* 1 (2005): 711–18.

———. "The City That Haunts: The Uncanny in Fruit Chan's *Made in Hong Kong.*" In *Between Home and World,* edited by Cheung and Chu, 352–68.

———. "Dialogues with Critics on Chinese Independent Cinemas." *Jump Cut: A Review of Contemporary Media,* no. 49 (2007). www.ejumpcut. org.

———. "*Durian Durian*: Defamiliarisation of the 'Real'." In *Chinese Films in Focus II,* edited by Chris Berry, 90–98. Hampshire and New York: A BFI book published by Palgrave Macmillan, 2008.

——. "Introduction: Cinema and the City at a Moment of Danger." In *Between Home and World*, edited by Cheung and Chu, 248–71.

——. "The Hi/Stories of Hong Kong." *Cultural Studies* 15, no. 3/4 (2001): 564–90.

Cheung, Esther M. K., and Chu Yiu-wai, eds. *Between Home and World: A Reader in Hong Kong Cinema*. Hong Kong: Oxford University Press, 2004.

Chion, Michel. *The Voice in Cinema*. Edited and translated by Claudia Gorbman. New York: Columbia University Press, 1999.

Chow, Rey. "A Souvenir of Love." In *Ethics after Idealism: Theory, Culture, Ethnicity, Reading*, 133–48. Bloomington: Indiana University Press, 1998.

Chu, Blanche Wing-Ki. "The Ambivalence of History: Nostalgia Films as Meta-Narratives in the Post-colonial Context." In *Between Home and World*, edited by Cheung and Chu, 331–51.

——. *The Representation of Space in Contemporary Hong Kong Nostalgia Films*. M.Phil. thesis. Hong Kong: Chinese University of Hong Kong, 1998.

Corrigan, Timothy. "The Commerce of Auteurism: Coppola, Kluge, Ruiz." In *A Cinema without Walls: Movies and Culture after Vietnam*, 101–36. London: Routledge, 1992.

Debord, Guy. *The Society of the Spectacle*. Translated by Donald Nicholson-Smith. New York: Zone Books, 1995.

de Certeau, Michel. *The Practice of Everyday Life*. Translated by Steven F. Rendall. Berkeley: University of California Press, 1984.

Derrida, Jacques. *Specters of Marx: The State of the Debt, the Work of Mourning, and the New International*. Translated by Peggy Kamuf. New York and London: Routledge, 1994.

Dissanayake, Wimal. "The Class Imaginary in Fruit Chan's Films." *Jump Cut: A Review of Contemporary Media*, no. 49 (2007). http://www.ejumpcut.org.

——. *Wong Kar-wai's Ashes of Time*. Hong Kong: Hong Kong University Press, 2003.

Drakakis-Smith, D. W. *High Society: Housing Provision in Metropolitan Hong Kong 1954 to 1979: A Jubilee Critique*. Hong Kong: Centre of Asian Studies, University of Hong Kong, 1979.

Foucault, Michel. "The Eye of Power." In *Power/Knowledge: Selected Interviews and Other Writings, 1972–1977*, edited by Colin Gordon, translated by Gordon, Leo Marshall, John Mepham, and Kate Sopher, 146–65. New York: Pantheon Books, 1980.

Freud, Sigmund. "The Uncanny." In *The Standard Edition of the Complete Psychological Works of Sigmund Freud*, Vol. XVII, translated by James Strachey et al., 224–25. London: Hogarth Press, 1964.

Fung, May. "i-Generations: A Tentative Study" (in Chinese). In *i-Generations: Independent, Experimental and Alternative Creations from the 60s to Now*, edited by Hong Kong Film Archive, 4–7. Hong Kong: Leisure and Cultural Services Department, 2001.

Gan, Wendy. *Fruit Chan's Durian Durian*. Hong Kong: Hong Kong University Press, 2005.

Gordon, Avery F. *Ghostly Matters: Haunting and the Sociological Imagination*. Minneapolis: University of Minnesota Press, 1997.

Hannerz, Ulf. "Cosmopolitans and Locals in World Culture." In *Global Culture: Nationalism, Globalization, and Modernity*, edited by Mike Featherstone, 237–51. London: SAGE Publications, 1990.

Hansen, Miriam. Foreword to *Public Sphere and Experience: Toward an Analysis of the Bourgeois and Proletarian Public Sphere*, by Oskar Negt and Alexander Kluge, ix–xli. Minneapolis: University of Minnesota Press, 1993.

Harvey, David. "From Managerialism to Entrepreneurialism: The Transformation in Urban Governance in Late Capitalism." In *The City Cultures Reader*, edited by Malcolm Miles, Tim Hall, and Iain Borden, 50–59. London: Routledge, 2000.

Hjort, Mette. "Danish Cinema and the Politics of Recognition." In *Post-theory: Reconstructing Film Studies*, edited by David Bordwell and Noel Carroll, 520–32. Madison: University of Wisconsin Press, 1996.

Hjort, Mette, and Sue Laver. *Emotion and the Arts*. New York and Oxford: Oxford University Press, 1997.

Hjort, Mette, and Scott MacKenzie, eds. *Purity and Provocation: Dogma 95*. London: BFI, 2003.

Ho, Sam. "The Hong Kong Indie: New Times, New Art." *Cinemaya: The Asian Film Quarterly*, nos. 61–62 (2003–04): 4–9.

Hsia, C. T. *The Classic Chinese Novel: A Critical Introduction*. New York: Columbia University Press, 1968.

Hung, Ho-fung. "Rediscovering the Rural in Hong Kong's History: Tankas, Hakkas, Puntis and Immigrant Farmers under Colonialism." *Hong Kong Cultural Studies Bulletin*, nos. 8–9 (1998): 2–16.

Jameson, Fredric. *The Cultural Turn: Selected Writings on the Postmodern, 1983–1998*. London and New York: Verso, 1998.

Jenks, Chris. "Watching Your Step: The History and Practice of the *Flâneur*." In *Visual Culture*, edited by Stephen Jenks, 142–60. London: Routledge, 1995.

Kermode, Frank. *The Sense of an Ending: Studies in the Theory of Fiction*. New York: Oxford University Press, 1967.

Keung, John K. "Government Intervention and Housing Policy in Hong Kong: A Structural Analysis." *Third World Planning Review* 7, no. 1 (1985): 23–44.

Klawans, Stuart, Annette Michelson, Richard Peña, James Schamus, and Malcolm Turvey. "Round Table: Independence in the Cinema." *October* 91 (2000): 3–23.

Kleinhans, Chuck. "Independent Features: Hopes and Dreams." In *The New American Cinema*, edited by Jon Lewis, 307–27. Durham and London: Duke University Press, 1998.

Knabb, Ken, ed. and trans. *Situationist International: Anthology*. Berkeley, Calif.: Bureau of Public Secrets, 1981.

Kristeva, Julia. *Strangers to Ourselves*. Translated by Leon S. Roudiez. New York: Columbia University Press, 1991.

Kwitko, Ludmilla. *Local Manifestations and Global Linkages: The Political Economy of Public Housing in Hong Kong*. Ann Arbor, Mich.: U.M.I., 1990.

Lam, Connie. "Hong Kong Independent Scene in the 90s." In *The Age of Independents: New Asian Film and Video*, edited by Bobo Lee, 3–4. Hong Kong: Leisure and Cultural Services Department and Hong Kong Arts Centre, 2000.

Law Kar. "An Overview of Hong Kong's New Wave Cinema." In *At Full Speed: Hong Kong Cinema in a Borderless World*, edited by Esther C. M. Yau, 31–52. Minneapolis: University of Minnesota Press, 2001.

———. "The Significance of *The Arch*." In *A Comparative Study of Post-War Mandarin and Cantonese Cinema: The Films of Zhu Shilin, Qin Jian and Other Directors*, edited by Urban Council, 163–65. Hong Kong: Urban Council, 1983.

Lee, Bono. "*Made in Hong Kong* and the Experience of Public Housing Estates" (in Chinese). *City Entertainment*, no. 482 (1997): 54.

Lefebvre, Henri. *The Production of Space*. Translated by Donald Nicholson-Smith. Oxford: Blackwell, 1991.

———. *Writings on Cities*. Edited and translated by Eleonore Kofman and Elizabeth Lebas. Oxford: Blackwell, 1996.

Leung, Ping-kwan (Yesi). *Hong Kong Culture* (in Chinese). Hong Kong: Hong Kong Arts Centre, 1995.

Levy, Emanuel. *Cinema of Outsiders: The Rise of American Independent Film*. New York and London: New York University Press, 1999.

Li, Cheuk-to. "Introduction." In *Phantoms of the Hong Kong Cinema*, edited by Urban Council, 9. Hong Kong: Urban Council, 1989.

———. "*Young and Dangerous* and the 1997 Deadline." In *Hong Kong Panorama 96–97*, edited by Urban Council, 10–11. Hong Kong: Urban Council, 1997.

Lim, Bliss Cua. "Spectral Times: The Ghost Film as Historical Allegory." *Positions* 9, no. 2 (2001): 287–329.

Long Tin. *Post-1997 and Hong Kong Cinema* (in Chinese). Hong Kong: Hong Kong Film Critics Society, 2003.

Lui, Tai-lok. "Home at Hong Kong." In *Changes in Hong Kong Society through Cinema*, edited by Urban Council, 88–92. Hong Kong: Urban Council, 1988.

McBeath, Graham B., and Stephen A. Webb. "Cities, Subjectivity and Cyberspace." In *Imagining Cities: Scripts, Signs, Memory*, edited by Sallie Westwood and John Williams, 249–60. London: Routledge, 1997.

Merritt, Greg. *Celluloid Mavericks: The History of American Independent Film*. New York: Thunder's Mouth Press, 2000.

Morris, Meaghan. "Transnational Imagination in Action Cinema: Hong Kong and the Making of a Global Popular Culture." *Inter-Asia Cultural Studies* 5, no. 2 (2004): 181–99.

Morris, Pam, ed. *The Bakhtin Reader: Selected Writings of Bakhtin, Medvedev, and Voloshinov*. London and New York: Edward Arnold, 1994.

Ng, Ho. "The Confessions of a Film Anarchist." In *Hong Kong New Wave: Twenty Years After*, edited by Provisional Urban Council, 55–59. Hong Kong: Provisional Urban Council, 1999.

Pang, Laikwan. *Building a New China in Cinema: The Chinese Left-Wing Cinema Movement, 1932–1937*. Lanham, MD: Rowman & Littlefield, 2002.

———. "Death and Hong Kong Cinema." *Quarterly Review of Film and Video* 18, no. 1 (2001): 15–29.

Rayns, Tony. "Made in Hong Kong." *Sight and Sound*, no. 8 (1999): 48.

Sek Kei. "The Wandering Spook." In *Phantoms of the Hong Kong Cinema*, edited by Urban Council, 13–16. Hong Kong: Urban Council, 1989.

Shih, Shu-mei. "After National Allegory." In *Visuality and Identity: Sinophone Articulations across the Pacific*, 140–64. Berkeley: University of California Press, 2007.

Stokes, Lisa Odham, and Michael Hoover. *City on Fire: Hong Kong Cinema*. London and New York: Verso, 1999.

Stringer, Julian. "'Your Tender Smiles Give Me Strength': Paradigms of Masculinity in John Woo's *A Better Tomorrow* and *The Killer*." In *Between Home and World*, edited by Cheung and Chu, 437–58.

T., Susanna. "No Future! No Future! Fruit Chan Speaks about *Made in Hong Kong*." In *Hong Kong Panorama 97–98*, edited by Provisional Urban Council, 54–57. Hong Kong: Provisional Urban Council, 1998.

Tambling, Jeremy. *Becoming Posthumous: Life and Death in Literary and Cultural Studies*. Edinburgh: Edinburgh University Press, 2001.

Taylor, Charles. "The Politics of Recognition." In *Multiculturalism: Examining the Politics of Recognition*, edited by Amy Gutmann, 25–73. Princeton, N.J.: Princeton University Press, 1994.

Teo, Stephen. *Hong Kong Cinema: The Extra Dimensions*. London: BFI, 1997.

Thompson, Kristin. *Breaking the Glass Armor: Neoformalist Film Analysis*. Princeton, N.J.: Princeton University Press, 1988.

Urban, Greg. *Metaculture: How Culture Moves through the World*. Minneapolis: University of Minnesota Press, 2001.

Vidler, Anthony. *The Architectural Uncanny: Essays in the Modern Unhomely*. Cambridge, Mass.: MIT Press, 1992.

——. *Warped Space: Art, Architecture, and Anxiety in Modern Culture*. Cambridge, Mass.: MIT Press, 2000.

Warner, Michael. "Publics and Counterpublics." *Public Culture* 14, no. 1 (2002): 49–90.

Williams, Raymond. *Marxism and Literature*. Oxford: Oxford University Press, 1977.

Wollen, Peter. "The Auteur Theory." In *Film Theory and Criticism: Introductory Readings*, edited by Leo Braudy and Marshall Cohen, 519–35. New York: Oxford University Press, 1999.

Xiao Bai. "The Indie's Search for Space within the Commercial Institution" (in Chinese). *City Entertainment* 615 (2002): 36–41.

Yau, Ching, *Filming Margins: Tang Shu Shuen, a Forgotten Hong Kong Woman Director*. Hong Kong: Hong Kong University Press, 2004.

Yau, Ka-fai. "3rdness: Filming, Changing, Thinking Hong Kong." *Positions* 9, no. 3 (2001): 535–57.

——. "Cinema 3: Towards a 'Minor Hong Kong Cinema'." *Cultural Studies* 15, nos. 3–4 (2001): 543–63.

Yue, Audrey. "*In the Mood for Love*: Intersections of Hong Kong Modernity." In *Chinese Films in Focus: 25 New Takes*, edited by Chris Berry, 128–36. London: BFI, 2003.

Zhang, Yingjin. *Chinese National Cinema*. New York: Routledge, 2004.

Zhang, Zhen. "Building on the Ruins: The Exploration of New Urban Cinema of the 1990s." In *The First Guangzhou Triennial: Reinterpretation: A Decade of Experimental Chinese Art (1990–2000)*, edited by Wu Hung et al., 113–20. Guangzhou: Guangdong Museum of Art: Art Media Resources, 2002.